# Praise for Leading Through Fire: Resilient Leadership for People, Planet, and the Future

Bold, brilliant, and deceptively simple, *Leading Through Fire: Resilient Leadership for People, Planet and the Future* is the book we all need as we face increasingly complex challenges. Davis offers us a clear path forward inspired by personal stories, scientific research, and global examples rooted in nature and community. After reading, I felt lighter and more joyful, affirmed in my leadership and inspired to take courageous new steps.

*Ilsa Govan*
*Co-Founder of Cultures Connecting and author of What's Up with White Women? Unpacking Sexism and White Privilege in Pursuit of Racial Justice*

In a world that can at times feel so overwhelming, Brenna's book has found a way to cut through to the heart of so many of our problems, by providing a blueprint for all leaders, and aspiring ones, on how best to lead to best achieve your desired results with compassion, resilience and grace.

By embracing imperfection, compassion and nature, Davis has created a pathway for so many of us who are feeling overwhelmed by the immense challenges of it all to find clear, grounded and purpose based leadership techniques to make a more positive difference in our jobs, schools, communities and even within our own families.

*Kevin Wilhelm*
*CEO, Bestselling Author, and Teacher*

Brenna Davis offers a vision of leadership that integrates lessons from non-human nature and the best of human nature. In Leading Through Fire, she makes space for the harrowing parts of leadership, reframing them as powerful lessons that inform our evolution. I'm deeply grateful for this voice as we collectively redefine leadership to mean far more than power.

*Rachel Budde*
*Founder and CEO, Fat and the Moon*

Do you hear the call of leadership, or the call to broaden and expand your leadership but hesitate, as if you're being beckoned to walk barefoot over burning coals? Or you're comfortable with your role as a leader yet yearn for tips to tune up your leadership as a practice. Leading Through Fire: Resilient Leadership for People, Planet and the Future is the book for you. I've enjoyed the gift of Brenna Davis' experience- and evidence-base wisdom during many wide-open sessions over coffee and as a collaborating co-leader. Reading Leading Through Fire is the next best thing to hearing Brenna speak of compassion, communication, courage, and above all, purpose. And your mind will hum with the Reflection queries she provides.

*Kevin Scribner*
*Board Chair, Global Ocean Health*

This book is a wisdom council. Brenna provides guidance, creative solutions and feedback that keeps the heart aligned with the leadership values we need to remember. Messengers are alive on each page, invitations and conversations that embolden us to bring the greatest gift of any leader, the ability to learn and apply what is leaned to the greater good of local and global communities in order to heal the atmosphere that we all rely on.

This book is an active cooperation with a positive future for all.

*Char Sundust,*
*Spiritual Teacher, Author*

Brenna Davis has written the book every values-driven leader needs right now. Leading Through Fire: Resilient Leadership for People, Planet and the Future is equal parts inspiration, toolkit, and rally cry. With grounded wisdom and a voice that's both fierce and deeply human, Brenna names the challenges of our time without flinching—and then shows us how to lead anyway.

This isn't another book about leadership theory. It's a lived manifesto for purpose, resilience, and courageous action, rooted in real-world stories and hard-won lessons. Whether she's guiding us through a childhood memory of a clear-cut forest or into a boardroom decision with planetary impact, Brenna brings us back to what truly matters. The reflection questions are practical and profound—I found myself stopping often, not just to think, but to feel.

What I appreciate most is that Brenna doesn't preach from above—she walks beside us. She reminds us that we don't need to be perfect to lead; we need to be present, connected, and willing to show up with heart.

Highly recommend for anyone who wants to make a difference without burning out.

*Everett Considine*
*Transformational Coach*

Dynamic evolutionary leadership in today's world beckons us to stretch beyond comfort and what we think is possible. On that journey, the pages of Leading Through Fire: Resilient Leadership for People, Planet and the Future are likely to become one of your favored resources. With potential to ignite deeper insight around your contribution to our shared world, it's a must read. Brenna is an experienced, passionate, and knowledgeable guide sharing wisdom that transcends time. Whether you're leading one or many, the pearls in this book will simultaneously ground and embolden you in ways you can't yet imagine

*Emily Paul*
*Transformational Guide for Visionaries and Innovators*

Brenna has provided a gift, a book that provides important and distinct steps, a blueprint, for readers to reflect on while moving through a time of planetary upheaval and uncertainty in becoming courageous, and compassionate leaders. Each chapter introduces qualities on what I believe to make us exceptional human beings such as purpose, compassion, courage, diversity, and cooperation and illustrating how being in nature, finding joy in simple things will propel us through hard times.

Any book that quotes and pays tribute to Dolly Parton, the Dali Lama, David Bowie and ends with a quote by Joe Stummer from the Clash is my kind of book. Brenna is my hero!

*Lisa Damm*
*Angelic Reiki Master Practitioner, ACIM Facilitator and*
*Reader of Akashic Records*

*Leading Through Fire: Resilient Leadership for People, Planet and the Future* ignites the spark of change within each of us, inspiring us to incorporate new and better practices into our leadership journeys. Brenna's message encourages us to become leaders who can walk through fire, emerging resilient and even stronger. Her perspective highlights that joy is not a frivolous luxury but a vital leadership superpower—an essential foundation for uniting teams, especially during challenging times. She teaches us that fostering joy nurtures resilience, encourages collaborative problem-solving, and unlocks new possibilities.

Brenna's journey exemplifies the transformative power of authentic leadership grounded in compassion and joy. As we learn from her example, we are reminded that leading with heart and resilience can create ripples of positive change—making our world a better place, one courageous step at a time.

*Jan Schiffner*
*Who's Who in America, 4 times International Best-Selling*
*Author, Award Winning Market Sales Manager,*
*International Public Speaker, Podcast and Television Talk*
*Show Guest*

I0170635

# LEADING THROUGH FIRE

## RESILIENT LEADERSHIP FOR PEOPLE, PLANET, AND THE FUTURE

## BRENNA DAVIS

First Edition: June 2025
ISBN: 979-8-9989844-1-9
Printed in the United States of America

For inquiries about permissions, speaking engagements, or bulk purchases, please contact:
Lumination Hive, LLC
www.luminationhive.com
Portland, Oregon

Disclaimer:
This book is for educational and inspirational purposes only. The author shares personal experiences and leadership insights, but these should not be construed as professional advice. Readers are encouraged to reflect on their own circumstances and seek guidance as needed. The views expressed are those of the author.

*For leaders anytime and everywhere.*

*The future is unwritten.*

**— Joe Strummer**

# CONTENTS

# FOREWARD

I first crossed paths with Brenna Davis in 2021 during a women-based leadership anthology project that I curated. Even then, her voice stood out—calm yet courageous, grounded yet visionary. She spoke with clarity about what mattered most: people, the planet, and the kind of leadership that doesn't just respond to crisis but transforms through it.

Over time, it became clear that Brenna wasn't just contributing to important conversations—she was living them. Her leadership journey has never been about titles or trends. It's about integrity. It's about showing up, again and again, with fierce compassion, unwavering purpose, and the willingness to do the inner and outer work of leading through fire.

This book, *Leading Through Fire*, is a powerful extension of who she is. It's not theory—it's lived wisdom. Brenna invites readers into the very heart of what modern leadership demands: resilience, clarity, courage, and care. She gives us tools—practical ones—that help you realign with your purpose, make values-driven decisions under pressure, and lead with both strength and softness.

She doesn't shy away from the truth: these are fiery times. But what makes her message distinct is that she doesn't call for burnout or bravado. Instead, she calls for brave, creative, adaptable leaders—those willing to lead unapologetically and with vision, while also understanding the ripple effects of every choice on their communities, their teams, and future generations.

One of the most compelling aspects of this book is Brenna's deep reverence for nature—not just as metaphor, but as method. She reminds us that reconnecting with the natural world can ground our nervous systems, restore perspective, and reignite our leadership. Whether it's walking among trees or simply stepping outside to breathe, nature becomes a co-leader in our path forward.

She also urges us to embrace diversity—not as a box to check, but as a strategic advantage and moral imperative. She reframes courage as a daily practice, not a personality trait. She champions excellence, not perfection—knowing that real impact is found in momentum, missteps, and shared progress.

Behind every page is Brenna's commitment. This book wasn't dashed off on a whim—it was built with intention, care, and a deep sense of responsibility. She carried it with her while running a successful company, advocating for environmental sustainability, and mentoring others—all while carving out time to write, reflect, and refine this message.

*Leading Through Fire* is not just a book—it's a legacy. It is a timely call to lead with conviction and compassion. It offers not just hope, but a path forward.

May it inspire you, challenge you, and equip you to lead from a place of power, purpose, and peace.

Because the fire isn't going away. But neither is the leader within you.

With deepest gratitude,

Dr. Izdihar Jamil, Ph.D.

21x Bestselling Author | Visibility Expert | TEDx Speaker and Curator

www.izdiharjamil.com

SCAN ME

# WELCOME

# THE CALL TO RESILIENT LEADERSHIP

When I was a kid growing up in the Pacific Northwest, the forests felt endless. I spent hours running through mossy trails, looking for salamanders and treasures in the ferns. Those woods were my playground, my sanctuary. Back then, it felt impossible to imagine a world where forests might disappear or where the waters I waded into might grow too acidified to hold life.

But today, we are living that reality. Wildfires rage. Oceans warm. Species vanish. We are standing in a time of unprecedented change, and much of that change isn't for the better. And it's happening faster than we ever expected. From the rise of artificial intelligence to the escalation of climate chaos, our world is transforming more in a single lifetime than in entire centuries before. Some changes bring innovation. Many bring profound, life-altering challenges.

And in the middle of all of it, leaders are being asked to do something extraordinary: To keep leading anyway. If you're reading this book, it's because you feel that call. You're here because you care deeply about something: your team, your community, the planet we all share. You want to lead in a way that makes a difference, even when the path isn't clear, even when the fire is raging.

I wrote this book for you.

After more than two decades leading in sustainable business, I've learned this: Leadership in this time isn't about having all the answers. It's about staying rooted, resilient, and clear-hearted when the winds of change are howling. It's about learning to communicate with courage, to make brave decisions, and to lead through fire. You don't have to be perfect to do it. I'm not. None of us are. But we can be courageous. We can be intentional. We can lead in ways that create a better future for generations to come.

This book is a guide, a love letter, and a call to action. You'll find tools here to help you:

- Root yourself in purpose when the ground feels shaky.

- Lead with compassion, even when the stakes are high.

- Communicate with courage and make clear decisions under pressure.

- Embrace imperfection while still reaching for excellence.

- Build teams and communities that thrive on diversity and trust.

- Create momentum when the world tells you to stand still.

- Find joy even when the world feels heavy.

This book is designed to be a quick read with impactful, focused chapters that you can finish over your morning coffee. Each chapter ends with reflection questions designed to help you move from inspiration to action. Don't worry about doing it perfectly. Grab a journal, a napkin, or just a quiet moment. The important thing is to stay engaged, to keep moving, and to keep choosing leadership even when it feels hard.

The world doesn't need perfect leaders. It needs resilient ones. And the leaders who can stay rooted in purpose, lead with compassion, communicate with courage, take action with resilience, and hold onto joy will shape what comes next.

If you're reading this, you are one of those leaders. The time is now. And the future is still unwritten. Let's lead through fire and into the future together.

In Gratitude,

*Brenna*

# CHAPTER ONE

# FINDING YOUR TRUE NORTH: ROOTED IN PURPOSE

*Do your little bit of good where you are; it is those little bits of good put together that overwhelm the world.*

**— Archbishop Desmond Tutu**

I remember the day I first felt the spark of purpose. I was a scrawny, little, red-headed five-year-old, standing in front of what just a few weeks before had been a lush, green ecosystem full of ferns, moss, huckleberries, tiny insects, raven song, and exotic salamanders. I spent hours watching nature, becoming a part of it, and discovering friendship in its leaves, water, and creepy crawlers. But now the trees were gone, leaving huge, rough stumps and dusty brown ground. I felt a pang of sadness so strong it almost took my breath away. There was also disbelief, as if I were looking at another world. Everything around me seemed unnatural still. The ravens had fallen silent, unsure where to go next.

At that moment, I thought, *this isn't happening!* I wanted to scream out *Why?* So, I turned to my mom and asked, *"Why did they do this? Why did they cut down this beautiful forest?"* Without missing a beat, she said, looking out at what I saw, *"I am sorry, honey. This is how developers do it. It's how people do business."* (Sad but true, I now know.) But something deep inside of me pushed back. I wanted more. A better answer, a different way. That powerful moment planted a seed in my heart. And then, it grew into the driving force behind my purpose in life.

It's no surprise, then, that I went on to study environmental science and business. I was obsessed with why businesses made decisions that negatively impacted the environment. I even went where most people would not. I did an environmental internship in an oil refinery to better understand the decisions that businesses made.

To this day, a dedication to building a more sustainable and just business world drives me. I get up in the morning and think, "My coworkers and I are going to do some good today!" The excitement of creating a better future drives me. It's an endless well of energy that I can tap into. It keeps me rooted in the essential.

## PURPOSE (RE)DEFINED

You've heard about my purpose, but what is purpose, actually? A personal purpose is your own long-term goal that provides you with motivation and meaning. Your purpose can develop over time based on your interest, or it can come to light after a powerful experience. It is something you want to accomplish to make the world a better place.

Dolly Parton found her purpose in childhood learning, so she developed a program to give kids free books. Dr. Martin Luther King's purpose was to see a dream of racial equity come to life. One of my coworkers is focused on his family, and his purpose is to help build a better world for them.

Over the years, as a sustainable business leader and CEO, I have encountered and mentored countless people who found their own versions of my forest experience. Each experience is as unique as the next. No matter how they discovered their purpose, their understanding of it and how it arrived proves beneficial to them as leaders, in whatever way they chose to lead. When my friends and colleagues share their reasons for getting up and going in the morning, I think to myself, "Harnessing the energy behind *that* is how we lead through fire."

There's a mountain of evidence showing that living with purpose can lead to greater resilience and well-being. For instance, one study found that people with a strong sense of purpose tend to live longer and enjoy better health outcomes.[1] Meanwhile, researchers found that individuals who report greater meaning in life also experience higher levels of happiness and life satisfaction.[2] Another study discovered that a clear purpose is linked to fewer depressive symptoms and improved overall well-being.[3]

It's clear that when we feel deeply connected to something bigger than ourselves, we find the resilience to push through obstacles that might otherwise stop us cold. There is immense power in purpose, and it can break the molds and patterns that stifle and hold us back.

## CONNECTING WITH YOUR PURPOSE

Here's the thing. Purpose isn't something you chase or earn. It's not a job title, or something you need to prove. It's something you remember.

It lives in your heart. In the things that light you up, the questions that won't leave you alone, the quiet knowing that shows up when the noise dies down. In a world that moves fast and values performance over presence, it's easy to lose touch with that deeper knowing. We get busy. We get tired. We forget. That's okay. Coming

---

[1] Hill, P. L., & Turiano, N. A. (2014). Purpose in life as a predictor of mortality across adulthood. *Psychological Science, 25*(7), 1489–1496.

[2] Steger, M. F., Oishi, S., & Kashdan, T. B. (2009). Meaning in life and its socio-cultural implications. *The Journal of Positive Psychology, 4*(1), 6–16.

[3] Kim, E. S., Strecher, V. J., & Ryff, C. D. (2014). Purpose in life and use of preventive health care services. *Journal of Behavioral Medicine, 37*(6), 1170-1178.

back to your purpose just takes a little space. A little quiet. A little trust in yourself.

One of the simplest ways I return to my purpose is reflection. Taking a moment to breathe and remember your why is a powerful thing. And if you're feeling uncertain about your purpose, or if you just want to reconnect with it, try this:

Find a quiet spot. Somewhere you can just be for a few minutes. Close your eyes. Breathe in for four counts. Out for four counts. Do that a few times until you feel your shoulders drop and your nervous system settle.

Then, ask yourself:

- What are the three most important things to me in my personal life? In my work life? Why?

- What touches my heart?

- What breaks my heart about the world right now?

- Which issue speaks loudest to me at this moment?

- Given who I am and what I've lived, how might I help? What's one small, meaningful way I can show up?

Trust yourself. More often than not, an issue that you have a passion for will emerge. Your purpose doesn't have to be glamourous or monumental. It just has to be real. Let it be your compass. Let it grow and shift with you.

If you'd like to dive deeper, there's a link to a worksheet at the end of this book that you can use to facilitate your process.

## YOUR PURPOSE STATEMENT

We all have bright days and dark days. When you're on a roll and making an impact, it's easy to remember your "why." Why you do it. Why you get up in the morning. Why you care.

On those days, your purpose feels like the sun. It's visible, energizing, and generates passion. But on harder days, the clouds can roll in thick and heavy like a fall morning in Seattle. You can lose sight of your why just when you need it the most. That's why I developed a purpose statement to hang above my desk as a steady reminder. It helps me live intentionally, keeping my roots deep even when the winds of change are howling.

In *The 7 Habits of Highly Effective People*, Stephen Covey wrote that creating a personal mission statement is one of the most important investments we can make in our own lives. He described it as "connecting with your own unique purpose and the profound satisfaction that comes from fulfilling it." A mission statement, he taught, becomes like a personal constitution. It's something you can return to over and over again to realign yourself when the world gets noisy, chaotic, or confusing. It isn't about setting rigid rules for yourself. It's about building a foundation that can support your courage, your clarity, and your deepest commitments.

I couldn't agree more. Life will pull at you from a thousand directions. Leaders, especially, are constantly navigating pressures, expectations, and shifting landscapes. Without a clear sense of purpose, it's easy to get knocked off course and to forget why you started, to lose the thread of your own story. A purpose statement doesn't eliminate the storms, but it gives you a compass to find your way through them.

In my own statement, I keep it simple. I share both the what and the why:

*To heal myself and the planet so that future generations of all species survive and thrive.*

It's not fancy. It's not long. But it's mine. And on the hard days, it reminds me why I stay in the work, why I lead the way I do, and why it matters to keep going.

I also had the privilege of doing this exercise with a team. I invited everyone to write their own personal mission statement. It was powerful to hear each person's words. Some statements were bold and visionary; others were quiet and deeply personal. Listening to them reminded me that purpose lives differently in all of us — but when we give it voice, it has the power to connect, inspire, and strengthen a community in ways strategy alone never could.

Now it's your turn.

Write your purpose statement. There is no single right way to do it. Everyone works differently. Some people may write a few lines that feel like a poem. Some might paint an image. Some might record a voice memo, compose a song, or sketch something symbolic. Let your purpose live in whatever form feels most alive to you.

When you write, don't worry about making it perfect. Start by asking yourself:

- What matters most to me?
- What am I here to heal, protect, or grow?
- What future do I want to help create?
- What lights me up, even when life feels heavy?
- What legacy do I want to leave behind in the everyday lives I touch?

Your first draft might feel rough or uncertain. That's okay. Your purpose doesn't have to be crystal clear at first. It can unfold over time. What matters is beginning. Planting the seed. Tending it.

Once you have your statement, keep it somewhere you can see it. Return to it when you need strength, direction, or renewal. Let it become a conversation you continue to have with yourself. If you feel called, share it with others too. You might be surprised at how much hearing someone else's "why" can deepen your connection and ignite your shared work.

# COLLECTIVE PURPOSE

When it comes to organizations, generating, managing, and consistently communicating a clear, collective purpose is difficult. And takes more than simply placing a motivational poster on the wall. But it works when you have one. A well-defined, genuine company mission statement aligns the efforts of employees, guides strategic decisions, and ultimately creates a lasting impact within the organization and in the larger world. Just as an individual's sense of purpose fuels their resilience and drive, a company's collective purpose can become its north star. It is a force that unites teams, strengthens the company culture, and inspires meaningful action.

In my own experience, I've seen firsthand how powerful a shared mission can be. I worked with a team where everyone was deeply committed to the same vision. The company's purpose was clear: to create healthier, more sustainable products while driving positive social and environmental impact. That clarity made a difference. It wasn't just about hitting quarterly targets; it was about knowing that each task, each product launch, and each innovation contributed to something bigger.

This collective sense of purpose brought the organization together in ways that went beyond job titles and daily responsibilities. It created a shared identity. Team members were more willing to collaborate, solve problems creatively, and take calculated risks because they knew they were working toward a meaningful goal. They understood that their efforts weren't just benefiting the bottom line—they were helping to address larger issues like environmental sustainability, community health, and ethical supply chains.

# PURPOSE DRIVES RESILIENCE AND INNOVATION

During tough times, whether it's an economic downturn or an industry disruption, organizations with a well-defined purpose often find it easier to weather the storm. Employees who believe in the company's mission are more likely to stick around and remain motivated, even when the road gets rocky. The company's unified purpose reminds them of why they do what they do, and it helps them stay focused on long-term impact rather than short-term challenges.

A collective purpose also fosters innovation. When everyone is focused on a common goal, it's easier to identify new opportunities, experiment with different approaches, and embrace imaginative problem-solving. Teams become more open to exploring new ideas because they're working within a shared framework of values and priorities. They're not just innovating for the sake of it; they're innovating to move closer to their mission.

# THE RIPPLE EFFECT OF PURPOSEFUL ORGANIZATIONS

The impact of a company's collective purpose extends far beyond the organization itself. When businesses operate with a clear mission, they often inspire other companies, communities, and even consumers to think more critically about the decisions they make. A company that's deeply committed to sustainability, for example, might influence industry standards, which in turn encourages suppliers to adopt better practices and help consumers make more informed, ethical choices.

A strong, purposeful mission can have a long-term impact on entire markets and industry operations. Purposeful businesses serve as role models, demonstrating that it is possible to be profitable while also making a positive impact. They attract employees who are driven to make a difference, investors who value sustainability and ethics, and customers who want to align their values with their purchasing decisions. In this way, a company's collective purpose serves as a catalyst for change, not only within the organization but also outside of its walls.

A company's purpose isn't just about what it produces or how much revenue it generates. It's about how it makes people feel, the values it upholds, and the legacy it leaves behind. By defining and living its collective purpose, an organization can inspire a sense of belonging, drive meaningful innovation, and create a lasting impact that goes far beyond its balance sheet.

## KEY TAKEAWAYS

- **Purpose is your center.** When everything feels like it's spinning, having a clear sense of purpose helps you stay steady and focused. It's the compass that keeps you moving forward, even through uncertainty.

- **Your purpose is yours alone.** There's no right or wrong version of purpose. It doesn't have to sound lofty or perfect. It just needs to be true to what matters most to you.

- **The science backs it up.** Both research and real-life stories show that a sense of purpose boosts motivation, resilience, and overall well-being.

- **If you're not sure what your purpose is, that's okay.** You're not behind. It's something you can explore and uncover. Try journaling, use the Purpose Power Worksheet, or talk it through with someone who sees you clearly.

- **Write your purpose down for the hard days.** On the days you feel depleted or overwhelmed, your purpose statement can remind you why you're here. Let it be a touchstone that brings you back to yourself.

# REFLECT ON PURPOSE

- What are the moments in your life when you felt most aligned, alive, or deeply connected to something that mattered? What do they reveal about what you're here to do?

- When the path feels unclear or hard, how can you return to the deeper reason you started? What would it look like to let that purpose steady you?

- What small steps could you take to live more in line with what matters most to you?

- How does your sense of purpose ripple outward? Who benefits when you show up rooted in what you believe in?

- Have you noticed your purpose shifting or evolving over the years? What does that say about where you've been and where you might be headed?

- Is there something you've been holding onto (like an old story, fear, or expectation that you need to release in order to move forward with more clarity and heart?

- How might you support someone else in discovering or deepening their purpose? What would it mean to be that kind of leader, friend, or mentor?

# CHAPTER TWO

# THE HEART OF LEADERSHIP: COMPASSION IN ACTION

*If you want others to be happy, practice compassion.*
*If you want to be happy, practice compassion.*

## — The Dalai Lama

Years ago, I had the honor of visiting the Obama White House to speak to high-ranking officials about business efforts to fight climate change. After I went through tight security, I walked through the marble halls of the Eisenhower Building. It was as if the walls whispered stories. The alabaster stairs were grooved with wear from generations of leaders moving from floor to floor.

After I made my way to the meeting room, I eased into a group of officials waiting for the meeting to start. I introduced myself to the person next to me, a woman dressed in a sharp blue suit who had a background in national security. I asked her what she was most concerned about in terms of national safety and the possibilities of the future. She shifted in her chair, looked me in the eye, and said with restrained passion, "Well, wars are fought over resources. The shift in the climate will cause a shift in resources that will likely cause conflicts. A lot of people will suffer."

I already knew this was a fact, but when I heard her say it, my heart dropped. I pictured all those people suffering. I felt a deep sense of urgency—like I was peering over the edge of a crisis that needed more than just policy fixes. It needed compassion on all levels: compassion for ourselves so we don't crumble under the weight of leadership and empathy for those who are impacted by climate change, both now and in the future.

## SELF COMPASSION

Compassion, defined as the willingness to recognize and alleviate suffering, is a fundamental pillar of effective leadership. As leaders, particularly when leading through fire, we must have compassion for ourselves. We're constantly problem-solving, troubleshooting, listening, and mentoring. We deal with budget constraints, the excitement and burden of growth, and mentoring people who would rather not be mentored. Then add care for our family, spouse, and other daily stressors. Even the most committed leader may feel overwhelmed by the burden.

There is a tendency to be hard on ourselves, especially when we are not getting the results we want. Sometimes, this comes from an addiction to perfection (we will talk about this issue in a later chapter), while other times, it's the weight of knowing that so many people rely on us. It feels like nothing is ever enough. Like we'll never feel on top of things.

The reality is this: nothing is ever perfect, and the demands will never end. That's just the way it goes, and there is no changing it. But we can find compassion for ourselves, so we don't lose steam or our hope. Leading others is a tough job, and many people choose *not to lead* for that reason. If you have chosen to lead or want to in the future, know this: You have stepped up to support, grow, and build a team. This is down-in-it, absorbing, and, at times, depleting work. So, give yourself moments of compassion. You can do this through positive self-talk—encourage yourself, breathe, and make room for perspective. And ensure that you are taking care of your needs, like drinking enough water and allowing for downtime when you need it.

Real science backs this up. Researchers like Dr. Kristin Neff have shown that self-compassion helps us stay emotionally balanced. It reduces anxiety and depression by giving us permission to be human.[4] Studies also indicate that practicing compassion may lower stress hormones like cortisol.[5] If we're to keep going—if we're to show up day after day to fight for our planet, for what's right and just—we need the mental and emotional space and energy that compassion provides.

Self-compassion is essential to resilient leadership because if you've got nothing left in the tank, nothing left to give, then you can't fuel others.

## COMPASSION FOR OTHERS

Spiritual leaders know that compassion opens doors to deeper connections with others. And research agrees. One iconic study showed that compassion training could increase altruistic behavior, meaning we're more inclined to lend a hand and collaborate—two things that are mission-critical when tackling problems in a rapidly changing world.[6] On the leadership front, management researchers found that when leaders cultivate compassion, they create a more collaborative, trusting environment.[7] That's the kind of energy we need to tackle big problems and manage crises.

---

[4] Neff, K. D. (2011). *Self-compassion: The proven power of being kind to yourself.* William Morrow.

[5] Rockliff, H., Gilbert, P., McEwan, K., & David, D. (2008). Compassionate mind training for people with high shame and self-criticism: A pilot study. *Journal of Cognitive Psychotherapy, 22*(3), 243-254.

[6] Weng, H. Y., Fox, E. A., Shackman, A. J., & Stodola, D. E. (2013). Compassion training alters altruism and neural responses to suffering. *Psychological Science, 24*(7), 1171-1180.

[7] Fehr, R., Yam, K. C., & Dang, C. (2015). Compassion at work: A review of the literature and implications for future research. *Academy of Management Annals, 9*(1), 50-127.

Compassionate leaders acknowledge and address the fact that we are all human beings with struggles, emotions, and individual needs. Each individual is unique. We all have unique gifts and talents. Compassionate leaders listen, seek to understand, empathize with others' challenges, and try to take the "rocks out of the shoes" of their team. They are building trust in their team because they care, and that creates a strong foundation for creativity and innovation.

Team members are more likely to be honest about problems, suggest innovative ideas, and support one another, knowing that their leader genuinely cares for their well-being. There is real trust, and a culture of trust goes a long way.

Some leaders don't value compassion because they think it means leniency or a lack of accountability. That couldn't be further from the truth. A compassionate approach for all involved typically means setting clear expectations and having honest conversations about performance. People perform best when they feel supported, especially when the stakes are high. High standards coupled with compassion is a winning combination.

By blending empathy with accountability, you can ensure that while individual needs are met, organizational goals remain a priority. This balance creates an environment where success is measured by outcomes, sure, but also by the growth and well-being of the team.

## COMPASSION FOR THE FUTURE

Let's take this one step further. We live in trying times, to put it mildly, and the actions that we take today will impact many, many generations into the future. People we will never meet – our great, great, great, great grandchildren's lives will be impacted by the decisions we make today. We are all interconnected across time and space. Just think of the first combustion engine – the promise of easy transportation and energy was not in balance with the negative impacts we are experiencing now.

We need to ask ourselves: "What kind of world am I leaving behind? Who will benefit, and who might suffer, because of what I choose to do today?"

Compassion for the future is required whenever we create a technological or scientific breakthrough. We must remain vigilant about its potential risks. For instance, breakthroughs in artificial intelligence may solve some problems but open the doors to others. We must resist the allure of quick fixes without consideration of future impacts. Compassion for the future encourages us to invest in approaches that are thoughtful, inclusive, and sustainable. The choices we make today are the foundation upon which future generations build.

## CULTIVATING COMPASSION

How do you develop compassion when you're maybe not so good at it?

Well, first things first: practice some self-compassion. If your self-talk has gotten noisy and disjointed or harsh, then correct it. Talk to yourself like you would a very close friend that you love. Find ways to take care of yourself, like a morning routine. Before I get going with my day, I like to pray, stretch, read, and, when the muse visits, write a little, even if it's just to map out my intentions for the day. This helps me tend to my own needs compassionately so that I can tend to the needs of others. If you're looking for your own morning routine, check out the book *The Miracle Morning*. It's transformational.

Second, work on your active listening skills. One of the simplest ways to cultivate compassion is to *really listen* to someone else-- step inside their shoes and see their perspective. Seek to listen without formulating a response in your head. So many people don't feel listened to in the world. You can build trust and nurture connections just by truly listening to them. Active listening builds empathy—an essential foundation of compassion—and creates a path for you to understand the challenges, fears, and needs of the people you lead.

Third, grow your sense of curiosity. Do your best to stay out of judgment and move into understanding. Compassionate leaders approach situations with curiosity rather than judgment. They ask questions like, "What might this person be going through?" or "What can I learn about their perspective?" This mindset encourages humility and reminds you that everyone's experiences are unique. By avoiding assumptions and staying open to different viewpoints, you deepen your own empathy and create an environment where people feel safe expressing their authentic selves.

Next, compassion is a practice. It isn't a one-time do-good thing. Habitual compassion means taking thoughtful actions over and over again and in different ways. It might mean checking in on a team member who seems stressed or acknowledging a coworker's hard work, or it might look like flexibility when someone else is dealing with personal challenges. It's even just smiling or saying hello to someone in an elevator.

Finally, remember that compassion is an important part of building an organizational culture. When you demonstrate care and empathy, you're encouraging other team members to do the same. You can recognize and reward compassionate behavior. Create approaches that factor in compassion and well-being. A culture rooted in compassion leads to better collaboration, creativity, and strength.

# KEY TAKEAWAYS

- **Self-Compassion isn't optional. It's foundational.** Leading in today's world is no small task. The pressure can be intense, and it's easy to fall into self-criticism or burnout. Offering yourself grace, kindness, and space to breathe isn't indulgent. It's essential for showing up with strength and clarity.

- **Compassion creates the conditions for trust and creativity.** When leaders listen deeply, acknowledge challenges, and show care, it opens the door for people to feel safe. When people feel safe, they take risks, speak up, and create. Compassion isn't soft; it's a catalyst for innovation and collaboration.

- **Compassion includes accountability.** Being compassionate doesn't mean lowering the bar. It means holding ourselves to high standards with care and respect. It's the combination of empathy and clarity that builds truly resilient teams.

- **Compassion means thinking beyond the moment.** The choices we make today shape the world our children and grandchildren will inherit. Compassionate leadership includes future generations in the circle of care, asking not just "What works now?" but "What endures?"

- **Compassion is a daily practice.** It's about how we show up, listen, stay curious, and build cultures rooted in respect and care. Compassion is a leadership muscle, and it gets stronger each time we use it.

# REFLECT ON COMPASSION

- Can you recall a recent moment when you were too hard on yourself? What would it have looked like to respond with the same compassion you'd offer a close friend?

- What small, realistic practices could you build into my day to speak to myself with more kindness and patience?

- When you listen to others, are you truly listening to understand? Or are you preparing to respond? How would it shift things if you slowed down and just received?

- How did you last show up for someone who was struggling? What happened in that moment, and what did it teach you about connection and leadership?

- How can you hold people to high standards while still being caring and human? What does it look like to lead with both clarity and empathy?

- When you think about the future, what kind of impact do you want to leave behind, and what choices today help shape that?

- What would it take to build a culture of compassion where you work or lead? What's one change you could make this week that might ripple out in a meaningful way?

# CHAPTER THREE

# GROUNDED LEADERSHIP: FINDING STRENGTH IN NATURE

*Those who contemplate the beauty of the earth find reserves of strength that will endure as long as life lasts. There is something infinitely healing in the repeated refrains of nature—the assurance that dawn comes after night, and spring after winter.*

**— Rachel Carson**

As a child, I remember spending quiet mornings in the Pacific Northwest forest, where the world seemed to slow down just enough to hear the wind whispering through the trees. The park was teeming with old massive trees, majestic ravens, and bushy-tailed, opinionated squirrels. I stretched out on the mossy ground. The cool earth pressed against my back, while the soft green cushioned me like a mattress. The branches of the Douglas Fir and Western Red Cedar trees swayed in the breeze. The sweet, dappled sunlight filtered through the leaves, leaving playful patterns on the ground. Time stood still in those moments, as if the world had paused so I could experience the magic of nature.

I watched tadpoles wriggle in the small ponds, fascinated by their quick moves and exciting frog future. The water was calm and murky. It reflected the trees like a mirror. I visited the tadpoles day after day to check on their growth. Soon, they had little feet and started to crawl. I found a deep connection to the natural world in those hushed mornings in the park. I found friends in the forest. Not in the traditional sense, but in a deeper, unspoken way—companions that didn't rely on words for understanding. I felt accepted.

As I grew older, this love for the earth never diminished; it deepened. Year after year. And today, I still make time to spend in the forest. I settle into the quiet of the woods in search of chanterelles. To walk through the damp underbrush questing for nature's hidden treasures, the ones she so generously offers is grounding and meaningful. No words are needed. Nature is an old friend, always there and always ready to welcome me back.

## CULTURAL DETACHMENT FROM NATURE

As much as I am connected to nature, the world around me is not. The urban sprawl, the hungry ghost of consumption, and the constant buzz of technology asking you to consume media all contribute to a growing sense of disconnection from the earth. In many ways, our modern world has built a fortress around nature. We create nature reserves far from our homes and offices as if they are separate and distant. We rarely stop to consider the earth beneath our feet, the plants and animals around us, or the natural systems that sustain us. We seem to do everything we can to forget that we are nature.

Detachment from nature is a cultural issue woven into the fabric of the Western way of life. While indigenous cultures around the world are founded in an embrace of nature, the Western world has largely abandoned it. When modern cultures embraced the mechanistic thinking ushered in by industrialization, human beings separated themselves from the natural world. In thought and in deed. The result? A mindset that views the natural world as a resource to be exploited or utilized. And a way of thinking that ignores the interconnectedness and humanity's reliance on nature's processes and ecosystems.

As a trained environmental scientist and a sustainable business expert, I could write a row of books on the unintended and ignored consequences of industrialization and our lost connection with the earth. But let's take a quick look here. The earth has suffered significant degradation due to increased pollution, resource depletion, and habitat destruction. The widespread burning of fossil fuels has led to air pollution and contributed to global warming and the collapse of ecosystems. Deforestation for urban development and agriculture has further contributed to habitat destruction and the loss of biodiversity, with estimates suggesting that 60% of global wildlife populations have declined since 1970. Around one million species are currently at risk of extinction.

Water pollution from industrial waste and over-extraction of freshwater resources has harmed aquatic life and threatened water availability. Soil degradation, driven by industrial agriculture and mining, has further compromised ecosystems. The proliferation of synthetic chemicals, including persistent pollutants like PCBs, heavy metals, pesticides, and plastics, has resulted in chemical pollution that lingers in the environment and harms both wildlife and humans. Overconsumption, driven by mass production, has led to excessive waste and the depletion of finite resources. These environmental impacts have been exacerbated by the unequal distribution of pollution, with marginalized communities bearing the brunt of the harm.

We must regain our closeness to the earth to protect our home for future generations. We generally have the technical capacity to do it. We need to grow the collective will to do it.

And all this has led to a loss of traditional knowledge. Indigenous cultures, for example, live in a close relationship with the land, passing down wisdom about sustainable practices, harvesting, and respecting the earth's cycles. As modern, Western-influenced cultures have distanced themselves from nature, much of this wisdom is now forgotten. Without this collective knowledge, people are less inclined to prioritize sustainability. Without the shared responsibility that comes from this historical knowledge, we face the challenge of reconnecting and restoring balance with the environment.

## UNDERSTANDING INDIVIDUAL DETACHMENT FROM NATURE

Detachment from nature has had profound effects not only on the environment but on human beings personally. Richard Louv's concept[8] of "nature-deficit disorder" brings attention to the negative effects of being disconnected from nature, especially for children. Kids who spend less time in nature are more likely to experience attention disorders, depression, and anxiety.

This issue is growing as kids today have less unstructured outdoor play and more screen time. The importance of unstructured outdoor play has been overshadowed by the lure of screen time and indoor activities. This disconnection also affects adults, who feel the strain of being indoors and on screens. The anxiety, burnout, and stress are common now, with more people experiencing the detrimental health effects of prolonged indoor living and lack of interaction with nature. Let's be real - who doesn't know a friend with anxiety? Or have some sort of anxiety?

Conservation psychologists, including Louv, underscore this issue with a concept they call the "extinction of experience." This term refers to how people are losing the opportunity to engage with nature daily because of full-tilt urbanization. People no longer know what it's like to walk through a forest, listen to birdsong in the morning, or

---

[8] Louv, R. (2005). *Last child in the woods: Saving our children from nature-deficit disorder.* Algonquin Books.

feel the earth beneath their feet—they can't draw on this experience when the chips are down or the world seems too loud and out of whack. If we don't have any experience in nature, like I did as a kid, we are less likely to foster any kind of environmental awareness. This "extinction of experience" weakens our ability to empathize with the environment, making it harder to mobilize for conservation efforts. When nature becomes something distant, something that is "out there" rather than "here," we lose sight of the urgency needed to protect it. If human beings do not protect the environment, we lose the critical ecosystems that we rely upon to survive. Parks and public wild spaces should be viewed as critical to our species.

## CLOSER TO THE EARTH IS BETTER HEALTH

When we detach from nature, we also detach from one of the most important sources of physical health: the natural world itself. Research shows that people who spend more time outdoors experience better cardiovascular health, lower blood pressure, and improved immune function. Scientists and researchers also discovered that natural environments reduce cortisol levels while boosting our white blood cell count, which is essential for fighting off infections.[9] We miss that natural boost when we don't get outside.

Sedentary lifestyles are a direct result of modern technological advancements. As we spend more time indoors and glued to screens, we reduce the amount of time we spend engaging with our bodies in natural spaces. We can fix that.

Gardening, for example, is a simple practice that gets us outside, moving, and interacting with the earth. The physical activity involved in gardening—from digging to planting and weeding—promotes better physical health, and the benefits of being outdoors are

---

[9] Li, Q. (2010). Effect of forest bathing trips on human immune function. *Environmental Health and Preventive Medicine, 15*(1), 9–17.

compounded by exposure to natural light, which boosts our vitamin D levels.[10] Without this exposure, we miss out on a key nutrient that plays a role in everything from immune health to mood regulation. When you're working in the garden, you're also working with the soil. Exposure to soil's beneficial microorganisms, such as *Mycobacterium Vaccae*, can stimulate the immune system and increase serotonin levels, improving mood and immune function.[11] Gardening and soil-based activities are linked to increased relaxation and mental clarity, not to mention reduced inflammation, better circulation, and enhanced sleep quality. The physical activity involved in gardening promotes cardiovascular health, while exposure to natural light helps regulate the body's circadian rhythm.[12]

The "hygiene hypothesis" suggests that exposure to soil's diverse microorganisms can improve immune health by balancing the immune system and reducing the risk of autoimmune diseases.[13] Time spent with soil also fosters a stronger mind-body connection, encouraging mindfulness, a sense of accomplishment, and greater appreciation for sustainability.[14] Collectively, these benefits demonstrate the profound impact that time in nature, especially

---

[10] UC Davis Health. (2023, May). *3 ways getting outside into nature helps improve your health.* Cultivating Health Blog.

[11] Lowry, C. A., Hollis, J. H., de Vries, A., Pan, B., Brunet, L. R., Hunt, J. R., ... & Lightman, S. L. (2007). Identification of an immune-responsive mesolimbocortical serotonergic system: Potential role in regulation of emotional behavior. *Neuroscience, 146*(2), 756–772.

[12] UC Davis Health. (2023, May). *3 ways getting outside into nature helps improve your health.* Cultivating Health Blog.

[13] Rook, G. A. W. (2013). Regulation of the immune system by biodiversity from the natural environment: An ecosystem service essential to health. *Proceedings of the National Academy of Sciences, 110*(46), 18360-18367.

[14] Capaldi, C. A., Dopko, R. L., & Zelenski, J. M. (2014). The relationship between nature connectedness and happiness: A meta-analysis. *Frontiers in Psychology, 5*, 976.

interacting with soil, can have on overall well-being. There's no way around it; gardening is good for the soul.

# EVEN MORE RECONNECTION WITH NATURE

You're a part of nature. Rachel Budde, an herbalist and creator of Fat and the Moon herbal body care, often says: You are nature. Reconnecting with it doesn't have to be complicated. It can be as simple as stepping outside, feeling the soil beneath your feet, and taking a moment to really notice the world around you. Maybe it's watching the birds fly by, observing the trees sway, or just standing barefoot on the soft grass or sand—it's all about being present at the moment.

Life gets busy—we're often working at desks, running errands, or just relaxing indoors—but nature is always there, ready to welcome us back. Whether it's a walk in the park, a hike through the woods, or just sitting under the shade of a tree, nature has a special way of grounding us and making us feel more connected.

A powerful practice to help deepen your connection with the earth is grounding or "earthing." This is when you make direct contact with the earth's surface by walking barefoot. Grounding is believed to help balance your body's energy by neutralizing free radicals, and research has shown it can reduce inflammation, improve sleep, alleviate pain, and even calm your nervous system.[15] Taking off your shoes and feeling the earth beneath your feet is not just good for your body; it's also a chance to pause, slow down, and be mindful of the present moment.

---

[15] Chevalier, G., Sinatra, S. T., Oschman, J. L., Sokal, K., & Sokal, P. (2012). Earthing: Health implications of reconnecting the human body to the Earth's surface electrons. *Journal of Environmental and Public Health, 2012*, 291541.

You can also try forest bathing, also known as Shinrin-yoku, a practice from Japan. It's all about immersing yourself in the forest and simply being present in it. Take in the sights, sounds, and smells around you without any goal in mind—just let the forest calm and restore you. Studies show that spending time in the forest can lower stress, reduce blood pressure, and improve your mood. The natural oils released by trees, called phytoncides, are known to boost immune function and promote relaxation. When we spend time in the forest, we're not just resting our bodies—we're reconnecting with the earth's natural rhythms.

As for me, I love gardening. For all the reasons I've stated and because. Growing your own food invites you into the rhythm of nature. It teaches you patience, mindfulness, and gratitude. When you plant a seed and care for it, you're participating in an ancient practice.

But you don't have to get your hands dirty to connect with the natural world. You can be in nature by simply observing it more mindfully. I love sitting outside and taking in all the little details around me, whether it's watching the leaves rustle in the wind or seeing how the bees move between flowers. Taking time to notice the small things around you—like the texture of a leaf, the path a stream takes, or the patterns in the sky—can deepen your relationship with nature. This practice of mindful observation is a beautiful way to express gratitude and appreciate the life around you. It doesn't matter where you are—life is everywhere, waiting to be noticed. This small act can change how you experience the world, bringing more wonder and appreciation into your daily life.

Getting closer to the earth and reconnecting with it means actively participating in its preservation. Whether it's volunteering for environmental organizations, helping with clean-up efforts, or making sustainable choices in your own life, you can play an important role in protecting the earth. Knowing that your actions are making a difference—whether it's planting trees, reducing waste, or supporting ethical businesses—gives you a sense of purpose and fulfillment. Being a steward of the earth means you're personally involved in its health and future. It's a reminder that our actions—both big and small—have lasting impacts, and through mindful efforts, we can help preserve and protect the planet for generations to come.

## CLOSER TO THE EARTH IS BETTER FOR TEAMS

Encouraging your work or business team to spend more time in nature can do wonders for workplace performance. Simple activities like taking outdoor breaks, going for a walk, or even holding walking meetings can help boost creativity, reduce stress, and improve focus. Bringing nature into the workplace—like adding plants or creating small green spaces—creates a calming atmosphere and encourages productivity. Practices like grounding—where your team walks barefoot on grass or soil—are fun things to incorporate into a team retreat. Planning team-building activities outdoors, whether it's a picnic or a retreat in nature, can help build stronger relationships. You can even encourage outdoor mindfulness activities, such as forest bathing or time in nature, to help your team recharge.

Supporting a sustainable work environment by promoting eco-friendly habits and providing healthy, organic food options strengthens the team's connection to the planet. By fostering a workplace culture that values time in nature, you can improve your team's performance, nurture mindfulness, and support the health of both your team and the planet.

## CLOSER TO THE EARTH IS BETTER FOR BUSINESS

Our business choices and decisions can also reflect a healthier relationship with the earth, one that creates a better future for all. It's not just a moral imperative - it's good business. Companies that recognize the profound interconnectedness between their organization and the planet are more likely to thrive.

When I first started working in sustainability, one of the big conversations was always around how to make the business case for it. That was partly because, years ago, the courts made it clear that companies are expected to maximize profits for shareholders. (We'll get into that a bit more later.) But here's the good news: over time, we've seen that companies that prioritize environmental sustainability tend to perform better—not just in impact but in profitability and overall success. They're often more efficient, waste less, and build stronger relationships with customers who care about the same things. These are the companies that are showing up as leaders—earning trust, growing their market share, and attracting both consumers and investors who want to be part of something better.[16]

While more mainstream companies are making strides toward sustainability, the green economy is already booming. In the UK, industries focused on climate solutions—like clean energy, sustainable construction, and electric vehicles—grew by 10% in 2024. Together, they added £83 billion to the economy and created nearly a million good-paying jobs. Not only is this sector growing fast, but the average wages are also well above the national average—showing that doing the right thing for the planet can be good for workers and businesses alike.[17]

In the U.S., clean energy isn't just growing—it's becoming a major force in our economy. By 2023, nearly 3.5 million people were

---

[16] Eccles, R. G., Ioannou, I., & Serafeim, G. (2014). The impact of corporate sustainability on organizational processes and performance. *Management Science, 60*(11), 2835-2857.

[17] CBI Economics & Energy and Climate Intelligence Unit. (2025). *The future is green: The economic opportunities brought by the UK's net zero economy.* https://ca1-eci.edcdn.com/250224-ECIU-CBIE-2024-Net-Zero-Economy-FINAL.pdf

working in green industries like renewable energy, energy efficiency, and clean transportation. These businesses aren't just doing good for the planet—they're creating jobs, sparking innovation, and proving that sustainability and profitability can go hand in hand.[18]

The future's looking bright for businesses that care about the planet—and Gen Z is a big reason why. This is a generation that isn't just talking about climate change; they're demanding action. In a global survey of over 10,000 young people aged 18 to 25, 41% said climate change is the biggest issue we face, and another 36% pointed to pollution.[19] And they're not sitting on the sidelines. From the School Strike for Climate to local clean-up efforts, Gen Z is showing up in massive numbers, inspired by voices like Greta Thunberg, to push for a better, more sustainable future.

And it's not just about protest signs—it's showing up in what they buy. A 2023 report found that 82% of consumers are willing to pay more for products with sustainable packaging, and that number jumps to a whopping 90% for Gen Z. Even more impressive? 71% of Gen Z shoppers have made a purchasing decision based on sustainability in the past six months. And 80% are actively seeking products with refillable packaging.[20] This is a generation that's voting with their dollars—and they're casting their vote for the planet.

At the heart of it all, this chapter is really a love letter—to the forests that raised us, to the soil that still steadies us, and to the future we're shaping together. Reconnecting with nature isn't a luxury or a side

---

[18] Environmental Entrepreneurs. (2023). *Clean Jobs America 2023*. E2. https://cleanjobsamerica.e2.org/

[19] Ipsos MORI. (2019). *Future of humanity survey*. Amnesty International. https://www.amnesty.org/en/latest/press-release/2019/12/climate-change-ranks-highest-as-vital-issue-of-our-time/

[20] Trivium Packaging. (2023, April 24). *2023 Buying Green Report: New data reveals consumers increasingly choose products in sustainable packaging globally, despite rising prices*. PR Newswire. https://www.prnewswire.com/news-releases/new-data-reveals-consumers-increasingly-choose-products-in-sustainable-packaging-globally-despite-rising-prices-301804273.html

note—it's a return to who we are. Whether you're leading a team, building a business, or just trying to move through life with a little more purpose, turning toward the earth can anchor you in clarity, health, and meaning. In a world that often feels like it's burning—fast-moving, uncertain, and overwhelming—*leading through fire* means grounding yourself in what's real and life-giving. Nature isn't separate from us; it is us. And when we lead from that place of connection, we don't just help heal the planet—we remember how to come home to ourselves.

# KEY TAKEAWAYS

- **Caring for the earth is good business.** Sustainability is smart business. Companies that prioritize the planet often see stronger financial performance, deeper customer loyalty, and growth in fast-rising green sectors.

- **We've lost touch with the earth – and it shows.** As we've built a culture around consumption, concrete, and screens, we've also created a dangerous distance from the natural world. That separation has real consequences for our environment, our communities, and our own well-being.

- **Nature-Deficit Disorder is real (and it matters).** Richard Louv gave us language for what so many of us have felt: when we disconnect from nature, especially as kids, we lose more than fresh air. We lose resilience, focus, and emotional balance. The rise in anxiety, attention issues, and stress? It's all connected.

- **Nature is one of the best healers we have.** Time outside is good for soul and also your health. From lowering blood pressure and stress to boosting immunity, simple practices like walking barefoot, digging in the garden, or just sitting under a tree make a real difference.

- **Reconnection starts small.** You don't have to live in the woods to reconnect. Step outside. Breathe deeply. Watch the way the light moves through the trees or notice the pattern of the clouds. These small, mindful moments help bring us home to ourselves.

# REFLECT ON NATURE

- When was the last time you truly felt connected to the natural world? What simple practice could help you return to that feeling more often?

- How does spending time outdoors shift your mood or energy? What patterns have you noticed in your body or mind when you spend time in nature?

- What are small, meaningful ways you can bring more nature into your daily routine—whether that's stepping outside with your morning coffee, tending a plant, or taking a walk without your phone?

- Have you ever tried walking barefoot on the earth—on grass, soil, sand? What would it feel like to let the ground hold you, even for just a few moments?

- If you garden or forage or simply get your hands in the dirt, what have those moments taught you about patience, rhythm, or your place in the world?

- What details in nature catch your eye or spark a moment of wonder? How might you build a habit of noticing them more intentionally?

- How does caring for the planet align with your sense of purpose? Where do you feel called to do more?

# CHAPTER FOUR

# BEYOND PERFECTION: THE ART OF EMBRACING EXCELLENCE

*If I waited for perfection...*
*I would never write a word.*

**— Margaret Atwood**

Like most people, after I graduated from college, I started on the bottom rung of the ladder. As a junior Environmental Scientist at a consulting firm, the work was tedious. It was just me and the data I collated and input. From my humble cubicle, I stared at spreadsheets that seemed to go on forever. Thousands of environmental monitoring data points, and my task: enter even more. And do it quickly and accurately. I worked long hours, entering the data and double-checking as I went. I wanted everything to be perfect.

After one of these blitzes of data entry, the project manager, in his buttoned-down shirt and khaki pants, waltzed over to my cubicle. In no uncertain terms, he told me that he was disappointed with my work. He found a handful of errors – four or five out of probably thousands – and wasn't happy. He expected perfection, and I did too. I felt deflated. I was committed to getting the data correct, but I had failed. If only I had tried harder, been more careful, and spent more time. Those thoughts spun through my head long after the conversation ended.

Looking back now, I see that moment through a different lens. I realize the project manager's frustration was misplaced. The real problem wasn't my attention to detail. It was the expectation that I, or anyone, could be flawless. I wasn't a machine. Perfection wasn't just unreasonable; it was impossible. Now I know that what that situation really required was a quality review process that acknowledged our shared humanity—a process that embraced excellence rather than demanding perfection. If we had built in a simple quality check, we would have caught those four or five errors. Together. And without anyone getting shamed or feeling inadequate.

## THE COST OF PERFECTION

Angeles Arrien, a cultural anthropologist, studied indigenous wisdom across multiple cultures worldwide, with a focus on spiritual traditions. Born to Basque heritage, her work synthesized insights from indigenous cultures around the world, including her own in Europe.

One of her primary goals was to bridge ancient wisdom with modern leadership, psychology, and personal development. In her research, she identified universal addictions that exist across cultures, one of which is the *addiction to perfection*. She observed that this addiction is particularly prominent in corporate success culture in the U.S. and in societies with rigid social expectations.[21]

Over the years, I have witnessed how perfectionism paralyzes individuals and teams, preventing them from acting, innovating, and even learning. I have worked with individuals who were afraid to share their work because it wasn't "perfect" yet, and I have seen

---

[21] Arrien, A. (1993). *The fourfold way: Walking the paths of the warrior, teacher, healer, and visionary*. HarperOne.

teams stall out because they refused to move forward until every detail was flawless. Ironically, these delays and hesitations only hinder progress.

The pursuit of perfection can quietly choke the very growth it's meant to encourage. While aiming high might seem admirable, perfectionism often shuts down creativity. When the fear of getting it wrong takes over, it stifles experimentation, learning, and innovation. These are the very things that help us grow and evolve as leaders and humans.[22]

It's natural to want to do things well—to put care into our work, to aim high, to get it "right." But perfection? That's a different story. Perfection is a moving target and chasing it can wear us down. Research shows that when we hold ourselves to rigid, unrealistic standards, we often fall into a loop of self-criticism and never feeling good enough.[23] It becomes less about doing our best and more about avoiding mistakes at all costs. But the truth is, real growth comes from trying, stumbling, learning, and adjusting. When we loosen our grip on perfection, we make space for something much more powerful: progress.

Perfectionism doesn't just affect how we work. It can deeply impact how we feel. While it might start as a drive to do well, unchecked perfectionism has been linked to serious mental health challenges, including anxiety, depression, obsessive-compulsive tendencies, and eating disorders.[24] One study even found that high levels of academic perfectionism among college students were associated with lower

---

[22] Stoeber, J., & Otto, K. (2006). Positive conceptions of perfectionism: Approaches, evidence, challenges. *Personality and Social Psychology Review, 10*(4), 295-319.

[23] Frost, R. O., Marten, P., Lahart, C., & Rosenblate, R. (1990). The dimensions of perfectionism. *Cognitive Therapy and Research, 14*(5), 449–468.

[24] Harvard Summer School. (n.d.). *The downside of perfectionism: How striving for flawlessness can harm mental health.*

psychological well-being and a greater risk of suicidal ideation.[25] As societal pressures to "do more" and "be perfect" continue to rise, younger generations are feeling this weight the most.

When we become fixated on getting everything right, we lose sight of progress and the power of learning from our mistakes. Instead of pursuing an unattainable standard, we should focus on *excellence*—a commitment to doing our best while embracing imperfections as part of the process. The most effective leaders, creators, and innovators understand that success is not about flawlessness but about adaptability, growth, and the courage to move forward despite uncertainty. Leading through fire requires knowing that meaningful progress lies not in being perfect but in being willing to learn, evolve, and keep going.

## CULTURAL WISDOM: EMBRACING FLAWS

Across cultures, various traditions embrace imperfection. People around the world created practices to help them remember that perfectionism is impossible and impractical.

In Japan, wabi-sabi is both an aesthetic and a philosophical concept. Rooted in Zen Buddhism, the concept of wabi-sabi values imperfection, impermanence, and simplicity. "Wabi" reflects an understated beauty of harmony with nature, while "sabi" honors the passage of time and the depth that the accumulation of years brings to objects and life. This philosophy finds beauty in things that are simple, weathered, and naturally aged, appreciating attributes such as asymmetry, rough textures, and imperfection. It is evident in Japanese traditions like kintsugi, the art of repairing broken pottery with gold to highlight its cracks rather than conceal them. Beyond

---

[25] Curran, T., & Hill, A. P. (2023). *Perfectionism is increasing over time: A meta-analysis of birth cohort differences from 1989 to 2021*. National Center for Biotechnology Information.

art, wabi-sabi is also a way of living. One that cultivates an appreciation for flaws and the aging process.[26]

There's a beautiful tradition in medieval Christian art and architecture that's stuck with me—one rooted in humility. Artisans, especially those building the great cathedrals like Notre-Dame, would sometimes leave intentional imperfections in their work. Not because they couldn't fix them but as a quiet acknowledgment that only the divine could be perfect. These small flaws were their way of saying, "We're human. We're not supposed to be flawless." It was a gesture of reverence and a reminder that beauty doesn't require perfection.

The Persian tradition of embracing imperfection is a part of its artistic, spiritual, and philosophical heritage. The intentional inclusion of small mistakes in Persian carpets reflects the belief that humans are not divine; therefore, our creations should not strive for absolute flawlessness. These intentional flaws, sometimes referred to as Persian flaws, appear as subtle variations in patterns or colors woven into the intricate designs of carpets.

This idea extends beyond textiles into Persian poetry, where imperfection and longing are central themes. Poets like Rumi and Hafiz wrote about the reality of human faults and flaws, our transience on earth, and a subsequent acceptance of these truths as a path to spiritual enlightenment. Rumi encouraged embracing change and imperfection:

*Be like a river*
*constantly flowing,*
*willing to erode its own banks*
*to discover new paths.*

---

[26] Juniper, A. (2003). *Wabi-sabi for artists, designers, poets & philosophers.* Stone Bridge Press.

*Be like the moon,*
*imperfect in shape,*
*yet full of light.*

*-Rumi*

Imperfection is not a flaw to be corrected but a natural and necessary part of life, creativity, and personal growth. Whether in art, philosophy, or spirituality, they invite us to embrace the beauty in coming up short or flailing in the face of life's demands.

## SOLUTIONS TO PERFECTION

The antidote to perfection, according to Angeles Arrien, is appreciation and acceptance. Instead of striving for an impossible ideal, we must cultivate gratitude for what *actually is* and recognize its beauty *as it is*. This allows space for our humanity: We can appreciate each other and ourselves for our unique approaches to life, and we can also accept that we all have talents and things in which we excel– and others in which we do not. And it's okay.

A driving force of perfectionism is the human tendency to think in extremes. Our minds convince us that it's either success or failure; it's either good or bad. The truth is that life doesn't play out in polar opposites. Usually, things are somewhere in the middle.

In cognitive behavioral therapy, psychologists help us reframe this perfectionism. Instead of thinking, "If this isn't perfect, I've failed," try telling yourself, "Doing my best is enough, and mistakes help me grow." This simple shift can make a huge difference in how you approach challenges and setbacks. The key is noticing those harsh, all-or-nothing thoughts and then replacing them with something more balanced and realistic.

Another way to break free from perfectionism is to practice self-compassion. If you wouldn't yell at a friend for making a small mistake, why do it to yourself? Dr. Kristin Neff, who we met in the last chapter, says treating yourself with kindness is one of the best ways to stop the perfectionist spiral. Instead of beating yourself up over something not being "good enough," remind yourself that it's part of being human. Try talking to yourself the way you would a close friend: Be encouraging and understanding rather than rigid and critical. Over time, practicing self-compassion can help ease the pressure to be flawless all the time.

Reframing mistakes as learning opportunities is another way to shift out of the perfectionist grind. If you're afraid to make mistakes, you're missing out on some of the best learning experiences. Dr. Carol Dweck's research on the growth mindset shows that people who see mistakes as part of the learning process tend to be more successful and resilient. Instead of seeing a mistake as proof that you're not good enough, try thinking like Thomas Edison, who thought of every failure as valuable feedback. Ask yourself, "What can I learn from this?" rather than dwelling on the mistake itself.

Author and personal growth guru Brené Brown, a shame researcher and author, posits that there is immense power in what she refers to as "good enough" thinking: giving yourself permission to show up and do your best without expecting perfection. Instead of getting stuck in the endless loop of tweaking and fixing, recognize that progress matters more than perfection. Think about it: Would you rather get something out into the world that's 80% done but valuable or spend years obsessing over making it "perfect" and never finishing it? The truth is, done is better than perfect. And, in most cases, what feels imperfect to you is still incredibly valuable to others. No art, no book, and no movie would ever be released if always waiting to perfect was how artists, thinkers, and pattern-breakers approached life. That includes this book (I know it's not perfect).

Life is about *taking* imperfect action. No one is ever truly ready. But the boots are by the door. So just put them on and take the first step. Perfectionism and procrastination go hand in hand because people often wait for the "perfect" moment, or the "perfect" skill set before they act. The problem? That moment never comes. Psychologists recommend adopting a "start before you're ready" mindset—just begin, even if things aren't perfect yet. Whether it's launching a project, speaking up in a meeting, or sharing creative work, taking small, imperfect steps builds confidence. Remember, action creates momentum, and you can always improve as you go. I think this is especially true for women, who were often taught that we had to be perfect before we even spoke up. Ignore that. Just start!

## A MORATORIUM ON TEAM PERFECTIONISM

All these lessons can be applied to your teams. Leaders need to create a culture where progress matters more than getting everything exactly right. Open communication and a sense of psychological safety let people share ideas and take risks without worrying about being judged. When mistakes are treated as learning moments instead of failures, it helps shift the mindset from fear to growth. Leaders can set clear expectations for quality while also reinforcing that improving over time is more important than nailing it on the first try.

One great way to avoid perfectionism is to build in regular feedback loops. Check-ins, peer reviews, and iterative deadlines give teams the confidence to keep moving, knowing they'll have chances to refine their work. Encouraging teamwork over isolated, perfection-driven efforts makes it easier for people to support each other and play to their strengths rather than getting stuck chasing impossible standards. By celebrating progress, recognizing effort, and staying flexible, teams can stay creative, resilient, and productive—without the stress of trying to be flawless.

Perfection might promise control, certainty, or safety—but it rarely delivers. What we need instead, especially in a world that feels like it's constantly shifting beneath our feet, is permission to be real. To lead with humility, to move forward even when things feel unfinished, and to trust that our best—flawed, evolving, learning—is enough. That's what *Leading Through Fire* is all about: showing up bravely in the heat of it all, not because we're perfect, but because we're present, committed, and willing to grow. The future doesn't need flawless leaders—it needs authentic and courageous ones. And that starts with embracing excellence over perfection every single time.

# KEY TAKEAWAYS

- **Perfection is a myth.** The idea of getting everything exactly right sounds noble, but it usually just keeps us stuck, stressed, and second-guessing ourselves.

- **Excellence leaves room for mistakes.** The best leaders aren't perfect. They are trying, learning, adjusting, and trying again.

- **Many cultures already get this.** From the quiet humility marks in cathedral stonework to the beauty of wabi-sabi, there's long-standing wisdom that reminds us that imperfection is part of what makes something meaningful.

- **Perfectionism hurts.** It's not just frustrating. It's exhausting. Research shows that perfectionism is tied to anxiety, depression, and burnout. It's not a high bar. It's a trap.

- **Progress matters more.** We don't need to wait until everything is perfect. Taking the next step, even if it's messy, is how real momentum (and real growth) happens.

# REFLECT ON PERFECTION
# (IMPRFECTLY SO!)

- When has perfectionism kept you from moving forward— either in your work or your personal life? What did it cost you, and what did you learn?

- Can you remember a time when you were afraid to make a mistake, and it held you back? What might have happened if you'd taken the leap anyway?

- How do you personally define excellence? And how does that feel different from chasing perfection?

- What small shift could you make this week to move from needing things to be flawless to simply letting yourself learn and improve as you go?

- Do any cultural or societal messages you've absorbed push you toward perfection? What would it feel like to gently let those go?

- Are there any stories or traditions (like wabi-sabi or kintsugi) that remind you that imperfection is part of beauty? How might you bring that mindset into your everyday life?

- Who is a leader or mentor you admire who embraces imperfection with grace? What does their example teach you about courage and trust?

# CHAPTER FIVE

# COURAGEOUS COMMUNICATION: SPEAKING TRUTH TO INSPIRE CHANGE

*I am convinced that courage is the most important of all the virtues, because without courage, you cannot practice any other virtue consistently.*

## — Maya Angelou

I still remember the morning I went on live television to talk about one of our boldest sustainability moves at PCC Community Markets. We had just launched a new sourcing standard for Chinook salmon— something that hadn't been done before in the grocery industry. We knew these salmon were critical to the survival of Southern Resident orcas, and we couldn't keep selling them without doing our part to protect the species. It was a hard call, but the right one. And that morning, sitting under those bright studio lights, I spoke from the heart about why we made the change. It wasn't just about seafood— it was about leadership, responsibility, and standing up for the ecosystems we all depend on.

I might have seemed confident under the lights. Not true. I was so nervous before going on air that I could barely think straight. My knees were shaking, and my heart was racing like I'd just sprinted up a mountain. I ducked into the bathroom moments before the segment, splashed cold water on my face, and stared into the mirror, trying to calm myself down. I kept thinking, *Just breathe. You know this. Speak from the heart.* And then I reminded myself—it wasn't about me. I was there to speak for the endangered orcas who had no voice, for the Chinook salmon they rely on, and for the ecosystems too often left out of the conversation. That grounded me. My heart was still pounding as I headed into the studio, but my purpose was clear.

Courage isn't about being fearless—it's about feeling the fear and choosing to show up anyway. Walking into that studio, facing the bright lights and cameras, took everything I had. But in that moment, I realized something important: courage is what gets things moving. It's the spark that ignites change—first in ourselves and then out in the world. And sometimes, all it takes is one shaky step forward to start a ripple.

## THE EVERYDAY PRACTICE OF COURAGE

Courage is sometimes defined as having the mental or moral strength to confront fear, difficulty, or uncertainty with determination and resilience. It's not the *absence of fear,* but instead, it is the ability to face challenges *despite fear.* When we are courageous, we move from feeling into action. It's not the easiest path, but it's the most impactful. We are courageous when we stand up to share our ideas, protect what we love, or challenge a status quo—even when we're worried about judgment or failure. Writing this book, for example, has been both exhilarating and terrifying. Putting my thoughts on paper—knowing some people might disagree or critique them—takes courage. But courage is a practiced skill, one that gets stronger each time we try.

Courage doesn't just help us power through tough moments, it actually helps us grow. Research shows that acting bravely can boost our confidence not just in the moment but over time.[27], and it doesn't stop there. Showing courage in challenging situations also has a ripple effect—it lifts our mood, strengthens our resilience, and even boosts the morale of the people around us.[28] That's the thing about courage: it's not just personal. It's contagious.

Pushing through your fear reminds you that you're more capable than you thought. And then that growing sense of self-assurance trickles into every area of life, from your relationships to your work. It's like lighting a candle in a dark room. Suddenly, you see possibilities where before there was only uncertainty.

## TRANSFORMATIONAL COURAGE

Courage doesn't just help us survive a tough moment. It helps us reimagine the world entirely. It's the bravery required to challenge the status quo, question outdated systems, and take bold steps toward a more just, sustainable, and compassionate future. Leadership, at its core, requires this kind of courage. Think of those who came before us. The people who fought for civil rights, clean water, safe working conditions, and ethical business practices. They didn't just navigate broken systems; they worked to transform them. And now, as the heat rises in every sense (climate, conflict, inequality), we're being called to do the same. The norms we once counted on are shifting, and the future will be shaped by those willing to lead with heart, clarity, and conviction. Fortunately, we're not starting from zero. We stand on the shoulders of those who lit the path before us. Now, it's our turn to carry that light forward.

---

[27] Rate, C. R., Clarke, J. A., Lindsay, D. R., & Sternberg, R. J. (2011). Implicit theories of courage. *The Journal of Positive Psychology, 2*(2), 80–98.

[28] Smith, E. M., Carter, J. A., & Hayes, L. J. (2017). Courage in organizations: A relational framework. *The Journal of Applied Behavioral Science, 53*(2), 249–277.

It's hard to imagine the kind of courage it took, but during the terror of Nazi Germany, a group of young people, many of them students in Munich, chose to speak up anyway. The atmosphere was tense, the streets watched, and speaking out came with real danger. Sophie Scholl and the women of the White Rose resistance quietly distributed leaflets, calling for people to resist the regime. They knew the risks. They knew what it might cost. But they believed that telling the truth was more important than staying silent. They leaned on each other for strength, and their quiet, determined bravery became a lasting reminder that real courage is often found in ordinary people doing the right thing—especially when it's hard.

Rosa Parks' decision to stay seated on that Montgomery bus wasn't just a moment of quiet resistance. It was an act of incredible courage. What many people don't know is that she had been involved in the civil rights movement for years before that day. In the summer of 1955, just a few months before her arrest, Ms. Parks attended a workshop at the Highlander Folk School in Tennessee. Highlander was a special place. It was an interracial school that trained people in how to stand up for justice using nonviolence and community organizing. While she was there, Ms. Parks learned practical tools for fighting unfair laws and built relationships with others who were just as committed to change. That experience helped strengthen her confidence and reminded her she wasn't alone. Her courage didn't come out of nowhere. It was rooted in preparation, community, and a deep belief in the power of collective action to bend the arc of history toward justice.

These brave women remind us that even in the darkest moments, individual and collective courage can spark real, lasting change. They show us that when we choose to stand up for what's right, especially when it's hard, we keep the light of truth, justice, and hope burning. That's what *Leading Through Fire* is all about: finding the strength to speak up, act, and carry forward what's good and lasting in the world, even when the heat is on. That kind of courage lives in all of us.

# COURAGEOUS DECISIONS

One of the most important qualities of a leader is the courage to make decisions. But let's be honest. In today's world, that's not always easy. The stakes feel higher, the risks are greater, and the path forward isn't always clear. Information can be unreliable, trends shift overnight, and what worked last year might not work tomorrow. One minute, you're navigating tariffs. The next, it's a change in regulations, or the sudden disappearance of an entire government agency. It's a lot. But even in the midst of that uncertainty, leaders still must choose a direction and move. And that takes real courage. Making decisions in this kind of climate means weighing the benefits, gathering information from diverse sources, and acting decisively and with compassion. And you'll need to prioritize a decision that's aligned with the purpose, ethics, and sustainability considerations of your organization or team.

Courageous decision-making isn't just an act of will. It's a leadership muscle we can all build. Research shows that leaders who regularly engage in courageous choices, especially when grounded in values and ethical clarity, are more likely to earn trust and inspire resilience within their teams.[29] Neuroscience also reminds us that fear and courage aren't opposites. They coexist in the brain.[30] So when we feel afraid and choose to act anyway, we're literally rewiring ourselves to be braver next time (think of me in the TV studio). That kind of purposeful action boosts our confidence over time and also strengthens team morale and helps create cultures where people feel

---

[29] Detert, J. R., & Bruno, E. A. (2012). Workplace courage: Review, synthesis, and future agenda for a complex construct. *Academy of Management Annals, 6*(1), 161–194.

[30] Mobbs, D., Hagan, C. C., Dalgleish, T., Silston, B., & Prévost, C. (2015). The ecology of human fear: Survival optimization and the nervous system. *Frontiers in Neuroscience, 9*, 55.

safe taking bold, thoughtful risks.[31] In uncertain times, that's exactly the kind of leadership we need.

During COVID, we all got our crash course in courageous decision-making. At the time, I was working in grocery. Our focus was clear: feed our community and protect the team that was making that happen. We found ourselves making big, high-stakes decisions every day. There was no time to second-guess. We'd wait for the latest guidance from the Governor, review the science, and then act fast to protect people. We sourced protective gear, rewrote protocols, worked to get vaccines, and backed each other up as we triaged an ever-changing situation. We didn't have perfect information, but we had each other—and we had the courage to keep moving forward, one decision at a time. I am sure that you have a similar story.

It doesn't take an emergency like a pandemic to make a courageous decision. Maybe it's a choice to go back to school. Or it's a choice to leave a career to focus on your family. It can even be deciding to change the focus of your business. These choices take courage, and the more small courageous decisions you make, like speaking up in a meeting or proposing a new idea to your team, the better you'll be at them.

## COLLECTIVE COURAGE

As leaders, whether we're guiding a company, a classroom, or a family, we have to be willing to have courageous conversations. That means stepping into moments that might feel uncomfortable, listening fully, and inviting others to speak honestly about what they see and feel. When we do that, we uncover the truth we need to make wise, well-rounded decisions. And once those decisions are made, we

---

[31] Hannah, S. T., Avolio, B. J., & Walumbwa, F. O. (2011). The locus of leader character: The role of courage and moral efficacy in ethical leadership. *The Leadership Quarterly, 22*(5), 979–993.

move forward together with shared understanding and a strong sense of alignment.

When people feel safe and encouraged to speak up, teams get stronger. The best ideas often surface when individuals know their input matters—especially during high-stakes moments. Inviting honest feedback helps us spot what's working, what's not, and where we need to pivot. It's not always easy, but when we lead with openness and curiosity, we create an environment where real innovation can take root and grow.

The Toyota Production System, or what many know as Lean, is a powerful example of how a leader can create a structure that encourages courage that fuels innovation. At the heart of it is a principle called *Kaizen*—the idea that everyone, no matter their role, is empowered to speak up and suggest improvements. It's about inviting people closest to the work to notice what's not working and offer ideas to make it better. When that kind of trust and participation is built into the culture, it not only strengthens the team—it drives real, lasting change.

Toyota thrives on a culture of courage, collaboration, and shared responsibility because employees feel heard and valued. The system supports regular feedback loops through consistent practices like daily stand-up meetings and visual boards on the shop floor. Both processes enable teams to quickly address issues, refine processes, and implement innovations. Workers see their suggestions lead to tangible improvements in efficiency, safety, and product quality. It gives them an avenue for courageous communication, and, as a result, they gain confidence, especially when they see their ideas successfully implemented on the shop floor.

Another great example comes from the airline industry. Specifically, the concept of Crew Resource Management (CRM) developed by NASA and later adopted by airlines around the world. Before CRM, flight crews were extremely hierarchical. Co-pilots or crew members often stayed silent even when they noticed a problem simply because the captain was considered the ultimate authority. Tragically, this dynamic contributed to several major accidents.

CRM changed that. It encouraged open communication, shared decision-making, and the belief that anyone on the team, regardless of rank, had not just the right but the *responsibility* to speak up if they had a safety concern. It transformed cockpit culture and significantly improved safety outcomes.

That's courageous conversation in action: building trust, flattening hierarchies when it counts, and creating conditions where people feel empowered to raise their voices even in high-stakes situations.

Processes like this, where leaders deliberately create space for courageous and honest conversations, are exactly what is needed in uncertain times. No one person can know the best solution every time. A team can find the most effective solution by bringing the best information to the table together. Building courage – and confidence – on your team is essential in today's world.

## COURAGE AS A PRACTICE

Courage isn't something we summon only in big, dramatic moments. It's something we build, little by little, every day. Like compassion, it's a practice. It's the quiet bravery of speaking up in a meeting, naming what feels off, or stepping into discomfort instead of avoiding it. It's saying the true thing when it would be easier to stay quiet. And yes, sometimes it's just showing up to that awkward networking event or raising your hand to speak in front of a crowd— even when your heart's pounding.

We all have different edges, but the work is the same: face the fear and move anyway.

Now is not the time to shrink back. The world needs steady, gutsy, grounded leadership. That means building your courage muscles before the fire is raging so when your moment comes to speak the truth, protect what matters, lead a team through crisis, or spark a movement, you're ready. You won't hesitate. You'll already have your boots on.

# KEY TAKEAWAYS

- **Courage isn't the absence of fear—it's choosing to act anyway.** Whether it's stepping onto a stage, into a boardroom, or into the fire of a tough conversation, courage starts with showing up, even when it's hard.

- **Everyday courage is how we prepare for the big moments.** Practicing small acts of bravery (speaking up, standing firm, telling the truth) builds the muscle we'll need when real pressure hits.

- **Transformational leadership takes boldness and heart.** The world doesn't change because we play it safe. It changes when we lead with integrity, purpose, and a willingness to challenge what's broken.

- **Courageous decisions build trust and momentum.** Even in uncertainty, moving forward with clarity and care helps your team feel grounded and inspired to act alongside you.

- **Brave conversations make teams and cultures stronger.** When people feel safe to speak up, offer ideas, and challenge respectfully, that's where the magic of collaboration and innovation really begins.

# REFLECT ON COURAGE

- When was the last time you did something even though it scared you? What did it teach you about yourself?

- Where in your life or work are you being called to speak up, even if it feels uncomfortable?

- How do you typically respond to fear? Do you freeze, overthink, avoid, or push through? What might help you choose courage next time?

- Who in your life has modeled courageous leadership for you? What qualities did they embody that you admire?

- What's one small act of courage you could take this week to build your "bravery muscle"?

- How does your team or community respond to honest feedback or bold ideas? What would help create more space for courageous conversations?

- What legacy of courage do you want to leave behind for your team, your family, or the world?

# CHAPTER SIX

# TOGETHER WE THRIVE: THE POWER OF DIVERSITY

*"I envision a future of work that looks something like this: people of all races, genders, sexualities, religions, and abilities are promoted on potential, paid equally, given the access and support they need to succeed, and respected to the fullness of their humanity."*

## — James D. White

Our planet is a diverse place: from plants and animals to human beings. The diversity of thought, perspectives, and experiences weaves a rich tapestry that has enabled our species to thrive. As I write this chapter, even acknowledgment of that fact is under a coordinated, planned attack. Federal employees have been directed to eliminate stories about diverse leaders from websites, grants to support underrepresented farmers have been eliminated, and funding has been cut for universities seeking to educate diverse students. All of this nonsense is weak, wrong, and harms the economic competitiveness of the country in the future. I have a passion for diversity. I am not an expert, but I share citations in this chapter that can help you dive deeper.

About five years into my career, I landed a job in a utility company working on environmental issues. No shock that the organization was led by white men from the Boomer generation. Let's just say saving the planet was at the top of most of these guys' minds. A counterpoint to that, I was a young female environmental scientist with a passion for health and safety. I started with big hopes of making a difference at the company, but the company culture drowned my voice and opinions. There were very few women. I was either talked over in meetings, or men repeated my ideas in meetings as their own. So, I clammed up. I subconsciously tried to make myself less different or noticeable. I wore plain, non-descript, and ill-fitting work clothes. I pulled my hair back into a bun. At night and outside the office, I transformed back into my true self – a punk rock girl with loose, wild hair and freely flowing views. Anyone who has been in my situation, that is, anyone in an underrepresented group and especially people of color, knows this scenario well.

At one point, a leader asked me to join an important meeting with a male colleague who was a peer. He was a bright light for me on the team—he always treated me with respect and was curious about my views. On the day of the meeting, we entered a bland, typical meeting room with a wall of old trade books from the 1970s, a whiteboard, and a dim fluorescent light above. At the table, there were several people already seated. I sat down next to my colleague, and a person next to him asked him in a proforma way: "How long have you had Brenna?" I was stunned. Without any forethought, this person assumed that I was my colleague's secretary. I was so grateful when my colleague corrected him and said: "Brenna is my colleague." The guy blanched, but no apologies were forthcoming. It was a moment that has stuck with me to this day.

Dr. Damon Tweedy wrote about his experience in his fantastic book *A Black Man in A White Coat: A Doctor's Reflection on Race and Medicine*. He recounts the times teachers and fellow students routinely assumed he was part of the janitorial staff while he sat in a medical school classroom waiting for class to start. Stereotypes like this sting when you've put years into studying to make it to medical school. That book was written in 2015, and still to this day, the problem persists. It goes without saying that compared to my situation as a white woman, his continues to be much more dire and life threatening.

## DIVERSITY AS A COMPETITIVE EDGE

If you're leading in today's world, you've got to bring different perspectives to the table. That's how you tackle complex problems and come up with the smartest solutions to build a better future for humanity and our companies. And it's not just the right thing to do. It's a real advantage. Great leaders know that diverse teams spark innovation, lead to better decisions, and actually boost the bottom line. When you've got people with different experiences and viewpoints, your team is quicker to adapt, better at spotting trends, and more likely to come up with creative answers. That bold statement has research to back it up.

Numerous studies reveal a strong correlation between diverse teams and improved business performance. The research indicates that teams with equal representation of men and women achieve higher sales and profitability compared to male-dominated teams. Teams ranked in the top quartile for gender diversity on executive teams are 39% more likely to outperform their industry peers in profitability.[32]

Ethnic diversity also plays a crucial role, with organizations that have the most racial and ethnic diversity being 27% more likely to achieve superior financial performance. Businesses that embrace diversity gain a competitive edge, leveraging a broader range of insights to navigate complex markets and emerging challenges.

Even at the highest levels of leadership, diversity drives success. A study of Fortune 1000 companies found a significant positive correlation between board diversity and the valuation of the

---

[32] McKinsey & Company. (2015). *The power of parity: How advancing women's equality can add $12 trillion to global growth.* McKinsey Global Institute.

company, highlighting that companies with diverse leadership teams make more effective strategic decisions and achieve stronger financial results. Businesses that embrace diversity gain a competitive edge, leveraging a broader range of insights to navigate complex markets and emerging challenges.

When teams lack diversity, they often succumb to groupthink or the tendency for a group to prioritize consensus over critical evaluation. In teams of people who are alike, dissenting ideas are more often dismissed, creativity is stifled, and blind spots are ignored. I've seen this happen in boardrooms and leadership meetings. In a rapidly evolving world, where businesses must address challenges like climate change, social inequities, and economic uncertainty, groupthink is more than just inefficient. It's a serious risk.

Diverse teams to the rescue. They are significantly better at tackling complex problems. Their varied experiences and viewpoints allow them to consider multiple angles, anticipate challenges, and develop strong, creative solutions. In contrast, teams that fail to embrace diversity risk falling behind, unable to adapt to the demands of an increasingly complex and interconnected world.[33]

## DIVERSITY SPARKS INNOVATION

We're living in a time of extraordinary challenges: climate change, social upheaval, rapid technological shifts. Solving problems like these isn't going to come from doing what we've always done. It's going to take fresh thinking, bold ideas, and the kind of creativity that only happens when people with different experiences come together.

---

[33] Homan, A. C., Van Knippenberg, D., Van Kleef, G. A., & De Dreu, C. K. W. (2007). Bridging faultlines by valuing diversity: Diversity beliefs, information elaboration, and performance in diverse work groups. *Journal of Applied Psychology*, 92(5), 1189-1199.

If you've ever been part of a team where everyone comes from a different background, you've probably felt it firsthand. The energy is different. New ideas spark more easily, conversations dig deeper, and solutions feel bigger and more original. Scott E. Page calls this "the diversity bonus"—the idea that cognitive diversity, or different ways of thinking, actually makes teams better at solving complex problems.

And the research backs it up. Researchers have found that teams made up of people from different backgrounds don't just come up with more ideas—they come up with better ones. In a large study of scientific collaborations, teams with greater ethnic diversity produced work that was more novel, more impactful, and had longer-lasting influence compared to more homogeneous groups.[34] When people with different experiences and ways of thinking come together, they challenge assumptions, uncover blind spots, and spark the kind of creative breakthroughs that move entire fields forward. Not only is this smartest strategy for innovation and success, valuing the diversity of your teams is the right thing to do

On the flip side, when teams lack diversity, they risk falling into an echo chamber where new insights are overlooked. Homogenous teams are more likely to reinforce existing perspectives rather than explore innovative solutions, reducing their ability to adapt and compete effectively.[35] Businesses that fail to adapt get left behind. (Just ask Kodak.)

The takeaway is simple: when you embrace diversity, you're not just making your team stronger—you're fueling the creativity,

---

[34] Freeman, R. B., & Huang, W. (2015). Collaborating with People Like Me: Ethnic Coauthorship within the United States. *Journal of Labor Economics, 33*(S1), S289–S318.

[35] Mannix, E., & Neale, M. A. (2005). What differences make a difference? The promise and reality of diverse teams in organizations. *Psychological Science in the Public Interest*, 6(2), 31-55.

adaptability, and innovation needed to meet this moment and shape the future.

## BANISHING BIAS

Humans evolved to make quick judgments about each other—a survival strategy that helped our ancestors rapidly assess threats and alliances in uncertain environments.[36] That instinct for fast thinking served an important purpose in the past, but today, it sometimes leads to unconscious biases: automatic attitudes or stereotypes that affect how we perceive, act, and make decisions, often without realizing it.

These biases are shaped over time by our life experiences, cultural messages, and societal influences. And they can show up in how we treat others—favoring someone who looks like us, assuming things based on someone's race, gender, age, or background, without meaning any harm. As Dr. Damon Tweedy powerfully described in his experiences, even well-intentioned people can fall into these patterns.

Here's the good news: everyone has biases, and there's a lot we can do about them. Awareness is the first step. Simply noticing—*"Hey, I just made an assumption about that person"*—opens the door to change. Tools like Harvard's Implicit Association Test (IAT) can help uncover hidden biases by measuring automatic associations between images or words and different groups.[37] I highly recommend trying it; you might learn something surprising about yourself.

Beyond awareness, bias work is a continual journey, not a one-time effort. There are excellent books, articles, and courses available that

---

[36] Cosmides, L., & Tooby, J. (1992). Cognitive adaptations for social exchange. In *The Adapted Mind: Evolutionary Psychology and the Generation of Culture* (pp. 163–228). Oxford University Press.

[37] https://implicit.harvard.edu/implicit/takeatest.html

can deepen your understanding of how bias shows up and what to do about it. The more you learn, the more you see, and the more consciously you can lead.

Mindfulness practices also support this work. Training ourselves to slow down and observe our automatic thoughts builds self-regulation and empathy, allowing us to recognize and adjust biased reactions in real-time.[38] Incorporating bias-correcting systems and mindfulness practices into daily routines improves self-regulation and empathy, helping individuals break automatic mental associations that fuel biases.

Another proven approach is perspective-taking: intentionally imagining yourself in someone else's shoes. Studies show that regularly engaging with people from different groups and consciously trying to see the world through their lens can gradually reduce bias over time.[39]

One way to practice this is simply by spending more time with people who aren't exactly like you. Another is by expanding what you read and experience. For example, I love science fiction, so I started mixing in Afro-Futurism books, exploring stories that center on Black and African cultural perspectives. Reading across different lived experiences helped me step into other worlds and ways of thinking, and it deepened my empathy in ways I didn't expect.

James White, former CEO of Jamba and co-author of *Anti-Racist Leadership,* interrupted bias by requiring a diverse slate of candidates for open roles. He also had white managers to attend Black and LatinX MBA conferences to increase the diversity of their networks

---

[38] Kalev, A., Dobbin, F., & Kelly, E. (2006). Best practices or best guesses? *American Sociological Review, 71*(4), 589–617.

[39] Kross, E., Ayduk, Ö., & Mischel, W. (2005). When asking "why" does not hurt. *Psychological Science, 16*(9), 709–715.

and give them a new perspective. He views managers as critical to bias interruption.[40]

Another way to catch bias before it sneaks in is surprisingly simple: slow down. When we're tired, rushed, or juggling too much, our brains naturally reach for shortcuts to save energy—and bias is one of those shortcuts.[41] It's not about being a bad person; it's just how our brains are wired when we're running on empty. Careful, thoughtful decision-making takes a little more time and effort. That's why giving yourself even a few extra moments to pause, breathe, and think--especially when you're making decisions about people—can make a huge difference. A little more space often leads to a lot more fairness.

Ilsa Govan and Tilman Smith, in their book *What's Up with White Women*, encourage us to prepare to commit to a continual process of uncovering our biases. Sometimes bias will show up in different areas of our life without warning and sometimes uncomfortably, but that's to be expected. They share that: "We must not only recognize our growth is an ongoing process but also have the internal motivation to seek out new information and try out new, often messy practices."[42]

Bias may be natural, but it's not inevitable. When we approach it with honesty, curiosity, and a commitment to keep learning, both individually and organizationally, we can build teams and communities where everyone has the chance to be seen, valued, and heard.

---

[40] White, J. D., & White, K. (2022). *Anti-racist leadership: How to transform corporate culture in a race-conscious world.* Harvard Business Review Press.

[41] Pendry, L. F., & Macrae, C. N. (1996). Stereotypes and mental energy: The influence of the perceiver's cognitive resources on the application of stereotypes. *Social Cognition, 14*(4), 330–354.

[42] Govan, I., & Smith, T. (2021). *What's Up with White Women?: Unpacking Sexism and White Privilege in Pursuit of Racial Justice.* New Society Publishers.

# YOUR OWN DIVERSITY COMMITMENT

At this point, it's clear that diversity is a necessity, not just for ethical reasons but also because it drives business success. Leaders who commit to diversity don't just passively support it. They actively champion it in every facet of their leadership. Your commitment to diversity starts with you. It's not just a decision; it's a responsibility, and it should be a core part of your leadership style.

One powerful way to solidify and communicate your commitment is by creating your own personal diversity statement. This statement should be a succinct declaration that defines your commitment to diversity as a leader, outlining how you will prioritize and foster an inclusive environment. For example, I wrote mine and made it public on my blog, and I encourage you to do the same. By creating and sharing your personal diversity statement, you're making a public commitment to uphold diversity, and this declaration serves as a personal accountability tool for the actions that follow.

A leader's diversity commitment shouldn't just be words on paper. It should guide your decision-making process. Your statement should reflect your values and outline concrete actions you'll take to create a diverse and equitable environment. This might include making sure all voices are heard, promoting diverse talent into leadership roles, or setting specific goals for diversity and inclusion initiatives.

It's also important to remember that a diversity commitment isn't static. As a leader, you'll constantly learn and evolve, and so should your diversity commitment. Whether it's by attending diversity training, reading diverse perspectives, or gathering feedback from your team, you should always be open to refining your approach to inclusion. Sharing your commitment with your team not only holds you accountable but also sets a tone for the organization, creating a ripple effect. When your team sees your genuine commitment to diversity and inclusion, they will be inspired to live out those values in their own work. As a leader, it's your responsibility to create an environment where every individual feels valued, heard, and empowered to contribute their unique perspectives.

## TEAM COMMITMENT TO DIVERSITY

Building a real commitment to diversity on your team starts with you. As a leader, people are always watching not just what you say, but what you do. It's the little things that build trust: making sure everyone's voice is heard in meetings, asking for different perspectives before making decisions, and keeping your door (and your mind) open to new ideas.

When you consistently show that you care about inclusion, it doesn't just stay a value. It becomes part of your team's everyday life. But here's the thing: good intentions aren't enough. If we want real change, we have to build better systems too.

Research shows that teams overcome bias most effectively when they put structures in place that make fairness the default, not the exception. For example, using clear, consistent criteria when hiring or promoting helps keep unconscious bias from creeping into important choices.[43] Teams that make the biggest difference don't just talk about diversity. They set goals, measure their progress, and hold themselves accountable.[44] It's about weaving inclusion into how you work every day, not just talking about it once in a while.

Next, it's key to create some clear goals. For example, you can make certain that diverse voices are included in important discussions or provide opportunities for people to share their thoughts. Create and grow an environment where everyone feels like they belong and can contribute. You also want to make sure everyone has equal access to

---

[43] Pendry, L. F., & Macrae, C. N. (1996). *Social Cognition, 14*(4), 330–354.

[44] Kalev, A., Dobbin, F., & Kelly, E. (2006). *American Sociological Review, 71*(4), 589–617.

growth opportunities. Just keep improving and building with inclusion top of mind, not an afterthought.

Lastly, building an inclusive culture requires ongoing work and feedback. One of the best things you can do is offer regular learning opportunities for your team, like training on unconscious bias or cultural awareness. Create spaces for open conversations where everyone feels safe sharing their ideas. Check-in with your team to see how they feel about your diversity efforts and adjust as needed. When you continue to be open, kind, and consistent in valuing diversity, you'll create a team that's not just stronger but also more creative, collaborative, and ready to take on any challenge together.

## DIVERSITY = THRIVING

Embracing diversity is essential for the success and sustainability of any organization. As a leader, your commitment to diversity becomes the cornerstone of your team's culture.

By actively addressing your own personal biases and creating a clear commitment to diversity in your leadership practice, you strengthen the fabric of your organization and set up your team to thrive in any circumstance. When massive challenges like climate change, social inequities, and economic uncertainties loom large, diverse teams are better equipped to navigate these complex issues.

Leading with diversity and inclusion isn't just a moral choice. It is a smart business decision that enhances creativity, drives innovation, and ensures long-term success. We have the power to shape a future in which everyone thrives.

# KEY TAKEAWAYS

- **Diversity fuels innovation and success.** Research shows that teams made up of different perspectives generate more creative solutions and outperform homogeneous teams in both decision-making and long-term impact. Diversity isn't just good for culture. It's a real competitive advantage.

- **Diversity is a business essential.** Beyond being the right thing to do, diversity is a smart strategy for growth. Companies with higher gender and ethnic diversity consistently perform better financially, with studies showing they are more likely to outperform their peers in profitability and innovation.

- **Commit to diversity personally.** As a leader, your personal commitment to diversity shapes the entire culture around you. Crafting and sharing a personal diversity statement, and living it every day, creates accountability and shows your team what truly matters.

- **Overcome personal bias with intention.** Recognizing and addressing your own biases is essential for building inclusive teams. By practicing mindfulness and using bias-correcting systems like blind recruitment, leaders can make fairer, more thoughtful decisions based on true merit.

- **Build a culture where every voice matters.** Creating an inclusive team culture means valuing diverse perspectives in every conversation and decision. Keep checking in with your team, seek honest feedback, and be willing to keep evolving your diversity efforts over time.

# REFLECT ON DIVERSITY

- When have you personally benefited from diverse perspectives—and did you fully recognize it at the time?

- What unconscious biases might you still be carrying, and how are they shaping your perceptions or decisions without me realizing it?

- How can you be more mindful in everyday moments, catching and questioning snap judgments before they take root?

- What specific steps can you take to actively seek out and experience different cultures, perspectives, and ways of life?

- How do you define diversity in your personal leadership and does that definition truly show up in how you move through the world?

- Where am you most comfortable and where might you intentionally step outside your familiar circles to keep growing?

- What ongoing practices, like reading, learning, traveling, or deep listening, can you commit to that will stretch your understanding and reduce your blind spots over time?

# CHAPTER SEVEN

# WINNING TOGETHER: COOPERATION FOR SHARED SUCCESS

*"A tree is not a forest. On its own, a tree cannot establish a consistent local climate. It is at the mercy of wind and weather. But together, many trees create an ecosystem that moderates extremes of heat and cold, stores a great deal of water, and generates a great deal of humidity."*

**— Peter Wohlleben, The Hidden Life of Trees**

I grew up with the smell of spices in the air and the sound of scoops clanking against big barrels of bulk foods. The Puget Consumer's Co-op—our co-op—wasn't just a grocery store; it was a community. My mom would take me by the hand, her flared jeans swishing as we walked down the aisles, past bins filled with grains and nuts, past people who knew each other's names.

Even as a kid, I could feel it. This place wasn't simply a place to buy food. It was a place for people to come together, a place where they pooled their resources to work toward something better. The grocery co-op was founded by folks who wanted access to healthier food at fair prices in a way that aligned with their values. It was about fairness. About sharing. And realizing that when we work together, we all win.

Nature already understands this. In a forest, trees don't just grow as individuals; they are part of an intricate, cooperative system. At the heart of this network are mother trees—older, deeply rooted giants that act as anchors for the entire ecosystem. Through underground mycorrhizal networks, they share nutrients and information with younger trees, helping them grow stronger. When one tree struggles, others send it what it needs. When a mother tree senses danger like drought, disease, and pests, it signals to the rest of the forest. The trees aren't competing; they're looking out for one another. Their survival depends on it. And so does ours. In a world that feels like it's burning, finding the win-win isn't just a hopeful idea; it's a necessity.

## INDIVIDUALISM AND ITS SHADOW

Yet cooperation hasn't always been at the center of the story we tell ourselves, especially in the West.

As an American child, I grew up surrounded by stories of rugged individualism—the lone cowboy, the self-made millionaire, and the belief that sheer determination is the key to success. We are indoctrinated into the idea that pulling yourself up by your bootstraps is the only way forward. But that's never been the whole truth. No one thrives in isolation. No one achieves success entirely on their own.

Individualism in Western culture, however, runs deep, and the story behind it is more complicated than we usually hear. It grew out of centuries of ideas, from ancient Greek philosophy to Renaissance humanism to Enlightenment thinkers like John Locke and Adam Smith. They argued that personal self-interest could somehow lift up all of society. But here's the catch: these ideas mostly reflected the experiences of a very specific group of people—wealthy, landowning, white men. Whole communities were left out of the vision from the very beginning: women, Indigenous peoples, enslaved Africans, and many others who weren't granted the same freedoms or opportunities.

Later, the Industrial Revolution pulled people away from small, interdependent communities and into growing cities. Traditional support systems like family networks, local relationships, shared resources, started to fray under the pressure of new economic realities.

And then came the rise of the "American Dream," telling us that anyone could climb the ladder through hard work alone. But what often got left out of that story was how uneven the playing field really was. And still is.

Today, more than 700 billionaires in the United States—over 80% of whom are white men—control a staggering $5 trillion in wealth, highlighting just how deeply opportunity and resources remain unequally distributed.[45][46] Meanwhile, about 26% of U.S. households spend 95% or more of their income on necessities, effectively living paycheck to paycheck, and that number rises to around 30% when using a 90% threshold for essential spending.[47]

## COOPERATIVE CULTURES: THRIVING TOGETHER

Thankfully, the individualist-at-all-cost poison has an antidote found in other cultures. That antidote is cooperation. Many cultures around the world operate on the principle of cooperation. Cooperation is

[45] Forbes. (2024, April). *The World's Billionaires List*. Forbes.

[46] Collins, C., & Flitter, E. (2024). *Billionaire Bonanza 2024: Mapping the wealth and power of U.S. billionaires*. Institute for Policy Studies.

[47] Bank of America Institute. (2024, March). *Living paycheck to paycheck: How lower-income households are navigating financial pressures*. Bank of America.

when we focus on the collective good over outcomes for just one person. In these societies that leverage cooperation, success is not measured solely by personal achievement but by the well-being of the group. Shared responsibility, reciprocity, and interdependence are the foundation of these cultures, creating resilient, sustainable, and deeply connected communities.

It's interesting that people from individualistic and collectivist societies activate different neural pathways when making cooperative decisions. While Western, individualistic cultures often approach cooperation in a goal-oriented way (seeking partnerships that mutually advance personal interests), more collectivist societies prioritize long-term relationships and group harmony.[48]

The Haudenosaunee Confederacy, also known as the Iroquois Confederacy, is one of the oldest known democratic systems in the world. Made up of six nations, their governance structure emphasizes consensus-building, long-term thinking, and shared responsibility. Decisions are made with the principle of the "seventh generation" in mind—considering the impact of any action on people seven generations into the future. This approach has allowed them to successfully steward land and resources for thousands of years.

A similar principle exists in many African cultures, particularly in the philosophy of Ubuntu, which is often translated as "I am because we are." Ubuntu is not just a philosophy; it is a way of life. It shapes decision-making, conflict resolution, and social relationships. Rather than viewing personal success as a solitary endeavor, ubuntu teaches that one's well-being is dependent on the well-being of others.

In Japan, they have long valued *wa*, or harmony. This concept influences everything from corporate culture to government decision-making. In business, consensus-building is crucial, and

---

[48] Kitayama, S., & Uskul, A. K. (2011). Culture, mind, and the brain: Current evidence and future directions. *Annual Review of Psychology*, 62, 419-449.

decisions are often made collectively rather than by a single authority figure, with balance and harmony in mind. Employees are expected to work together for the good of the company rather than prioritize personal ambition, a stark contrast to the individualistic competition seen in many Western workplaces.

Latin American cultures, while diverse, often emphasize *familismo*, a deep commitment to family and extended networks of support. In many Latin American communities, financial and emotional resources are shared among extended family members, and decisions are made collectively rather than independently. The concept of *compadrazgo*, or godparenthood, extends cooperative ties beyond blood relatives, reinforcing networks of mutual aid and responsibility.

Researchers Shinobu Kitayama and Ayşe Uskul found that people from individualistic and collectivist societies activate different neural pathways when making cooperative decisions. While Western, individualistic cultures often approach cooperation in a goal-oriented way (seeking partnerships that mutually advance personal interests), more collectivist societies prioritize long-term relationships and group harmony.

What these cultures show us is that there is more than one way to thrive. Individual success does not have to come at the expense of others. When cooperation is at the center of a society, it creates stronger communities, greater stability, and a more sustainable future. However, across all cultures, the human brain prioritizes social connection over isolation. Cooperation is not just a cultural construct; it is a biological imperative.

# THE NEUROSCIENCE OF COOPERATION

The human brain prioritizes social connection over isolation. Cooperation isn't just cultural. It's biological.[49] The question is not whether humans are naturally cooperative but rather why we sometimes struggle to cooperate.

When we collaborate, our brains release oxytocin, often called the bonding hormone. Oxytocin plays a key role in trust, social bonding, and generosity. It is why we feel good when we connect with others, why parents bond with their children, and why acts of kindness create a sense of warmth and fulfillment.[50] Higher oxytocin levels make people more likely to cooperate, trust others, and act altruistically.[51]

However, oxytocin is just one part of the equation. Cooperation also activates the ventral striatum, the brain's reward center, which releases dopamine, the same neurotransmitter that makes food taste good, music feel moving, and personal success feel satisfying.[52] When we work together, our brains *literally reward us* for doing so. Cooperation creates a feedback loop: the more we collaborate, the more we experience the neurological benefits of connection.

Another key to cooperation lies in mirror neurons, a type of brain cell that fires not only when we perform an action but also when we observe someone else performing that action. Discovered in the 1990s by neuroscientist Giacomo Rizzolatti, mirror neurons help us understand and internalize the emotions and actions of others.

---

[49] Kitayama, S., & Uskul, A. K. (2011). Culture, mind, and the brain: Current evidence and future directions. *Annual Review of Psychology*, 62, 419-449.

[50] Kosfeld, M., Heinrichs, M., Zak, P. J., Fischbacher, U., & Fehr, E. (2005). Oxytocin increases trust in humans. *Nature, 435*(7042), 673-676.

[51] Zak, P. J., Stanton, A. A., & Ahmadi, S. (2007). Oxytocin increases generosity in humans. *PLoS One, 2*(11), e1128.

[52] Rilling, J. K., Gutman, D. A., Zeh, T., Pagnoni, G., Berns, G. S., & Kilts, C. D. (2002). A neural basis for social cooperation. *Neuron, 35*(2), 395-405.

Imagine watching a friend take a sip of coffee. Your mirror neurons fire as if you were taking a sip yourself. This system is essential for empathy, cooperation, and social learning. It allows us to "feel" what others feel and then predict their intentions. This is why emotions are contagious and why cooperation often starts with simply understanding someone else's perspective.

When people work together, mirror neurons create a shared sense of purpose. This is why synchronized activities like dancing, singing in a choir, or rowing a boat in unison can create such powerful group cohesion. It is also why soldiers marching in step, sports teams training together, or even families cooking a meal side by side can feel deeply bonded. Our brains synchronize when we cooperate, making the act of working together *feel* fulfilling.

Much of what we think we know about human psychology and behavior was shaped by a narrow slice of the world's population. Anthropologist Joseph Henrich coined the acronym WEIRD (Western, Educated, Industrialized, Rich, and Democratic) to describe the populations that are most studied in psychology. These societies all emphasize independence and individual achievement, but it's worth noting that they are outliers in human history. Most human societies, Henrich's research shows, have prioritized cooperation, reciprocity, and shared success as key survival strategies. In many cultures, personal success is not seen as an individual pursuit but rather a collective effort, deeply tied to relationships and community.[53]

The implications of this research are profound. Competition is not inherently "natural," nor is individualism the default mode of human behavior. Cooperation is just as ingrained in us, if not more so.

---

[53] Henrich, J. (2020). *The WEIRDest people in the world: How the West became psychologically peculiar and particularly prosperous.* Farrar, Straus and Giroux.

# RECIPROCITY AND COOPERATION

Psychologists and economists have also studied cooperation using games for decades. One of the most well-known experiments is called the Prisoner's Dilemma. In one version of the game, most people choose to betray the other player, afraid of getting the short end of the stick. But when the game is played over and over, something shifts. Cooperation becomes the winning strategy. When people know they'll interact again, they start building trust, choosing collaboration over competition because they see the bigger picture.[54]

What is it that makes cooperation stick in these repeated interactions? It comes down to reciprocity: the simple idea that when someone treats us well, we will do the same.[55] Whether it's in friendships, business, or even diplomacy, we naturally mirror the behavior we receive. The more we interact with someone, the more we see patterns of trust and fairness emerge. In fact, studies reveal that when people believe their actions will affect future encounters, they tend to be more generous, fair, and willing to cooperate, not just for short-term gain but because they value the relationship itself.[56]

We see this play out in the real world all the time. Long-term business partnerships thrive on trust. Companies that build relationships with suppliers and clients based on fairness and reliability tend to perform better in the long run. Global cooperation works the same way. Nations that have a history of working together are more likely to keep their commitments, whether in trade agreements or

---

[54] Axelrod, R., & Hamilton, W. D. (1981). The evolution of cooperation. *Science, 211*(4489), 1390-1396. https://doi.org/10.1126/science.7466396

[55] Nowak, M. A., & Sigmund, K. (2005). Evolution of indirect reciprocity. *Nature, 437*(7063), 1291-1298. https://doi.org/10.1038/nature04131

[56] Fehr, E., & Gächter, S. (2000). Cooperation and punishment in public goods experiments. *American Economic Review, 90*(4), 980-994. https://doi.org/10.1257/aer.90.4.980

environmental policies.[57] Even in our personal lives, we gravitate toward people who consistently show up, reinforcing our instinct to invest in relationships that reward cooperation over time.

But what happens when trust breaks down? Unfortunately, even in repeated interactions, cooperation can fall apart, especially when people start feeling like others are taking advantage of them and running roughshod over their ideas and emotions. If someone repeatedly acts selfishly, ignoring the needs and opinions of others, those offended or dismayed may stop cooperating and shift into self-preservation mode.[58]

But this isn't the only way. The good news in all of this? When we create environments where trust is rewarded, cooperation bounces back. Whether through clear communication, accountability, or simply elevating fairness to standard operating procedure, we can rebuild the conditions that make working together the best choice.[59]

At its heart, game theory reminds us of something deeply human: we are wired to connect. The more we expect to see someone again, the more likely we are to be fair, kind, and cooperative because we know that our relationships shape our future. When we design systems, whether in business, government, or communities, that encourage repeated interactions, we're setting the stage for stronger, more resilient connections. And in a time when trust is in short supply, that's a lesson worth holding onto.

---

[57] Ostrom, E. (1990). *Governing the commons: The evolution of institutions for collective action.* Cambridge University Press.

[58] Trivers, R. (1971). The evolution of reciprocal altruism. *Quarterly Review of Biology, 46*(1), 35-57. https://doi.org/10.1086/406755

[59] Nowak, M. A., & Sigmund, K. (2005). Evolution of indirect reciprocity. *Nature, 437*(7063), 1291-1298. https://doi.org/10.1038/nature04131

# ECONOMIC COOPERATION: THRIVING TOGETHER

While large corporations often dominate economic conversations, cooperative economies have flourished for centuries, providing an alternative approach rooted in shared ownership, mutual support, and fair resource distribution. These models emphasize sustainability, equity, and long-term stability, ensuring that communities, not just shareholders, benefit from economic success.[60] Across the world, cooperative businesses have proven that financial prosperity and social responsibility can go hand in hand.

One of the most compelling examples is the Mondragón Corporation in Spain, Mondragon is a cooperative that has grown into one of the world's largest corporations. It employs a staggering 80,000 people— and counting! Established in the 1950s, Mondragón operates on principles of democratic decision-making and worker ownership. This means that profits are reinvested into the community rather than extracted for the benefit of a few. Employees actively participate in shaping company policies, fostering a culture of collaboration and fairness that challenges traditional corporate hierarchies. This approach demonstrates that businesses can thrive without exploiting workers or prioritizing short-term shareholder gains.

North of sunny Spain, those happy Danes in Denmark (Look it up! They're really happy.) have embraced cooperative housing, offering a model that contrasts sharply with speculative Danish real estate markets. Through cooperative housing structures, residents co-own their buildings and collectively decide on key issues such as rent, maintenance, and governance. This approach promotes long-term affordability, prevents displacement due to rising housing costs, and strengthens social bonds within communities. By focusing on collective well-being rather than profit maximization, Denmark's

---

[60] Birchall, J. (2017). *The governance of large co-operative businesses.* Co-operatives UK.

housing cooperatives provide a sustainable alternative to the volatile private housing market.

PCC Community Markets (the same Puget Consumers Co-op that I visited as a kid and eventually worked there) is the largest grocery cooperative in the United States. As a result of member ownership, the organization has been able to focus on its mission of organic and sustainable food systems. Its quality and ingredient standards have pushed the grocery industry further and kept countless toxic ingredients out of households in the Puget Sound region. Their activism also led to dozens of policies and laws that strengthened consumer protections, built organic agricultural standards, and started the careers of many new food entrepreneurs who otherwise wouldn't have found a place on the shelf.

Another emerging model in the United States that embeds cooperation into the core of business is the Perpetual Purpose Trust (PPT). Unlike traditional companies that are most often sold to the highest bidder, PPTs ensure that a business remains committed to its founding mission—whether it be environmental sustainability, worker well-being, or community investment—indefinitely. For example, Organically Grown Company transitioned to a Perpetual Purpose Trust to safeguard its mission of sustainable food systems. Patagonia is also a perpetual purpose trust focused on fighting climate change. This structure protects businesses from short-term profit pressures and aligns them with long-term social and environmental values.

These examples, from Mondragón to Denmark's housing co-op to the rise of Perpetual Purpose Trusts, illustrate that cooperation is not just a moral ideal but a proven economic strategy. By prioritizing shared success, sustainability, and long-term well-being, cooperative models challenge the rampant, misguided assumption that business success must come at the expense of people or the planet. If we hope to build a future that is both equitable and prosperous, then let's look to these models as blueprints for a more just and resilient economy.

# COLLABORATION AND MUTUAL AID

When a crisis happens, people come together. Time and again, in the face of war, natural disasters, pandemics, and economic collapse, communities have rallied, strangers have helped one another, and cooperation formed the foundation of their resilience.

Disasters, whether they are hurricanes, wildfires, economic downturns, or global pandemics, create a sudden and urgent need for cooperation. The structures of everyday life are disrupted, and people realize, often very quickly, that survival depends not on individualism but on working together. People form mutual aid networks, share resources, and support each other in ways that bureaucratic institutions often are unable to do.

One of the most striking examples of cooperation in crisis is the spontaneous response of ordinary people during and following natural disasters. In the aftermath of Hurricane Katrina in 2005, news reports focused heavily on looting and lawlessness, but sociological studies later found that the overwhelming response from the people of New Orleans was one of solidarity, not division. Neighbors helped neighbors, strangers rescued stranded families in boats, and community members created informal relief hubs in the absence of immediate government response. The same was true in Asheville, North Carolina, after they suffered the devastating damage of a rare inland hurricane nearly two decades later.

Following the 2010 earthquake in Haiti, grassroots organizations emerged overnight to distribute food, provide medical aid, and rebuild communities. Many of these efforts were led by local Haitians, not large international aid organizations. During the 2011 Fukushima nuclear disaster in Japan, thousands of elderly volunteers, calling themselves the "Skilled Veterans Corps for Fukushima," fearlessly offered to take on hazardous cleanup tasks. Their reasoning was simple: they were older and, therefore, more vulnerable to radiation's long-term effects, while younger workers still had long lives ahead of them. Scholars who have studied post-disaster recoveries note that the most effective relief efforts are often the ones driven by local communities, not outside interventions. Cooperation is most powerful when it is grounded in the people who know their communities best.

Historically, mutual aid has been a crucial strategy for marginalized communities facing systemic neglect. Black communities in the United States have relied on mutual aid networks for centuries, from the Underground Railroad to the civil rights movement to youth breakfast programs. Similarly, immigrant communities have long built informal support systems to navigate legal barriers, language obstacles, and economic exclusion. In times of crisis, these pre-existing networks become lifelines, demonstrating that cooperation is not just about short-term survival. It is about long-term resilience.

## COOPERATIVE LEADERSHIP

Mutual aid shows us what's possible when communities step up for one another. But how do we build that spirit into everyday leadership? It starts with shifting away from old-style, top-down leadership and embracing a more inclusive, service-oriented approach. *Servant leadership*, a concept introduced by Robert Greenleaf, flips the traditional leadership model on its head by focusing on supporting others rather than wielding authority. Servant leaders listen deeply, remove roadblocks, and ensure their teams have what they need to succeed. This kind of leadership creates a culture where people feel safe to share ideas, take initiative, and work together rather than compete against one another. Studies show that organizations with servant leaders tend to have higher employee satisfaction, stronger collaboration, and more innovation.[61]

Another crucial piece of the puzzle is *psychological safety*. A term coined by Harvard professor Amy Edmondson, psychological safety describes a work environment where people feel safe speaking up, making mistakes, and sharing ideas without fear of embarrassment or punishment.[62] When leaders create this kind of culture, teams are more engaged, creative, and willing to collaborate. Leaders incorporate this concept by encouraging open dialogue, modeling vulnerability (admitting when they don't have all the answers), and making it clear that mistakes are learning opportunities, not failures.

There are plenty of inspiring examples of cooperative leadership in action. Former New Zealand Prime Minister Jacinda Ardern put empathy and transparency first in her response to the COVID-19 pandemic. She focused on clear communication and collective responsibility rather than top-down control.

At the end of the day, leadership isn't about being the smartest person in the room. It's about creating an environment where *everyone* can contribute, feel valued, and work together toward something bigger than one person or one idea. The leaders who will shape the future won't be those who hoard power but those who build bridges, nurture relationships, and empower others. If we want stronger teams, more innovative workplaces, and more resilient communities, we need leaders who embrace cooperation. Not just because it's a nice idea, but because it works.

---

[61] Eva, N., Robin, M., Sendjaya, S., van Dierendonck, D., & Liden, R. C. (2019). Servant leadership: A systematic review and call for future research. *The Leadership Quarterly, 30*(1), 111-132. https://doi.org/10.1016/j.leaqua.2018.07.004

[62] Eva, N., Robin, M., Sendjaya, S., van Dierendonck, D., & Liden, R. C. (2019). Servant leadership: A systematic review and call for future research. *The Leadership Quarterly, 30*(1), 111-132. https://doi.org/10.1016/j.leaqua.2018.07.004

At its core, cooperation is an act of hope. It is a belief that together, we are greater than the sum of our parts. It is a commitment to the idea that no one should have to face hardship alone. Whether it is neighbors rescuing each other after a hurricane, strangers organizing food deliveries during a pandemic, or nations working together to prevent catastrophe, cooperation is the force that turns crisis into resilience. In a world facing unprecedented challenges, cooperation is essential.

## KEY TAKEAWAYS

- **Success has always been a collective journey.** Western individualism has often overshadowed the truth: no one achieves greatness alone. Success is built on shared resources, mutual support, and collective effort.

- **Our brains are wired for connection.** Neuroscience confirms that cooperation is more than just a nice idea. It's hardwired into us. When we work together, our brains reward us with trust, empathy, and a sense of fulfillment.

- **Cooperative models show us a better way.** Businesses rooted in cooperation, like co-ops and purpose-driven enterprises, prove that financial success and social responsibility can go hand in hand, creating long-term, sustainable prosperity for all.

- **Leadership that nurtures trust builds lasting success.** Leaders who prioritize psychological safety and foster collaboration create environments where teams are more engaged, innovative, and resilient. Leadership is about supporting others.

# REFLECT ON COOPERATION

- How has individualism influenced the way you approach success? Where might you find more joy and fulfillment by embracing cooperation?

- In which parts of your life do you notice competition getting in the way of collaboration? How can you invite more cooperation into those areas?

- What can you learn from nature's cooperative systems, like the way trees support one another? How can you bring that into your relationships and work?

- Has there been a time when cooperation led to a better outcome than competition? What was it about that situation that made cooperation work so well?

- How can you contribute to building more cooperative systems, whether in your workplace, community, or even with your family and friends?

- When things get stressful, how do you typically respond? Do you tend to go into self-preservation mode, or do you look for ways to collaborate? How can you improve your ability to work with others during tough times?

- What leadership qualities do you admire in others that make collaboration easier, and how can you bring those qualities into your own leadership style?

# CHAPTER EIGHT

# MOMENTUM MATTERS: CREATING CHANGE THROUGH ACTION

*"I was becoming, and they were waiting for me."*

**— Patti Smith**

There are so many moments in life where we feel like we should do something, but we hesitate. Instead of acting, we wait for permission, the perfect plan, or someone else to take the lead. But real change happens when people step up, even when the path forward isn't clear. One of my favorite examples of this is José Andrés, the world-renowned chef who founded World Central Kitchen (WCK). His story is a masterclass in taking action instead of waiting on the sidelines.

When Hurricane Maria slammed into Puerto Rico in 2017, it left the island in complete chaos—millions without food, water, or power. Governments and big relief organizations tried to mobilize, but the response was slow and tangled in bureaucracy. But José Andrés didn't wait for a plan or a perfect system. He just got on a plane, found a kitchen, and started cooking. He pulled in local chefs, organized volunteers, and, within days, built a meal distribution network that ended up serving over a million meals.

And here's the thing: he had no grand strategy mapped out. He didn't stop to ask, "Am I the right person for this?" or "What if I fail?" He just looked at what was needed and used the skills he had to take some action.

He figured things out as he went, adapting, problem-solving, and proving that momentum matters more than perfection. Today, WCK responds to disasters all over the world, from wildfires in California to the war in Ukraine, bringing food and hope to people when they need it most.

José Andrés didn't wait for permission. He didn't have a perfect plan. He just saw what needed to be done and got to work.

## BRINGING DREAMS INTO REALITY

What if he hadn't taken action? What if José Andrés had sat back and thought *someone else would figure it out*? What if, instead of stepping up in the face of disaster, he had let hesitation, logistics, or fear of failure stop him? Would thousands of people have gone hungry, waiting for help that never came?

Unrealized dreams have a way of lingering, don't they? They sit just out of reach, waiting for the perfect moment: the right time and circumstances or the right version of us to manifest. And yet, that moment rarely arrives. Instead, the dream stays where it is, as an idea, a possibility, a what-if that never gets the chance to unfold.

But dreams aren't just about us. More often than not, the dreams we carry, the ones that won't leave us alone, are calling us toward something bigger. They're clues, nudging us toward healing, not just for ourselves but for the world around us. Maybe that idea you keep pushing aside is the very thing that could restore a piece of the planet. Maybe the story you want to tell is the story someone else needs to hear to keep going. Maybe that business, that project, that bold move you can't stop thinking about is the one thing that could help heal a community or protect an ecosystem.

And yet, so many of us hold back. We hesitate. We wait until we feel ready. But here's the truth: you'll never feel 100% ready. There will always be uncertainty, always a reason to wait just a little longer. And in the meantime? The dream fades into the background while life moves forward.

I've felt it myself: the pull of hesitation, the temptation to play it safe. Because what if I fail? What if it doesn't work? But I've learned that the real risk is doing nothing. It's looking back years from now and realizing you never even tried. Dreams die from neglect. And when we let them go unanswered, we don't just lose a part of ourselves. We lose the opportunity to be part of something much greater.

Action is the only thing that separates an unrealized dream from a lived reality. You don't have to have it all figured out. You don't need permission. You just need to start. Take the messy, imperfect first step. Write the first page. Make the phone call. Launch the project. Because once you begin, momentum takes over. And suddenly, the dream that felt so distant is something you're actually living.

By writing this book, I'm choosing to share ideas, offer insights, and build future leaders who understand that while the path ahead may be fraught with challenges. I'm taking the first step. For me, writing has always been an act of rebellion against inaction.

The world needs people who are willing to take that first step. People who will choose action, even when it's hard or the result is unknown. Because the ones who do? They're the ones who make the future possible.

## UNDERTHINKING THE OVERTHINKING

Overthinking is a scourge, a pest that eats away at our productivity. It is that feeling of getting stuck in endless loops of planning, researching, and weighing every possible outcome until the moment for action has passed or is now dead in the water.

This stifling cycle of over-analysis often comes from fear. Common fears that most of us battle at one time or another in our lives. The fear of failure, making the wrong decision or looking foolish. And while taking time to think things through is important, there's a tipping point where thinking turns into avoidance. We tell ourselves we need just a little more information, a little more preparation.

Organizations often fall into the trap of endless meetings, overflowing reports, and five-year plans that remain stuck on the strategy deck. Meanwhile, the world continues to move forward, and valuable opportunities to make an impact slip away. As Bazerman and Moore point out in their research, the most successful leaders aren't those who get every decision right but those who make decisions, learn from them, and adapt as they go.[63]

The antidote to paralysis by analysis? Underthinking things. Action. Imperfect real-world action. Not reckless leaps but bold, thoughtful steps forward. Because no matter how much you plan, you'll never have all the answers in advance.

## PURPOSEFUL DECISIONS FOR A BETTER TOMORROW

While underthinking (avoiding the trap of over-analysis) can propel us into action, it's just one part of the equation. It's not enough to act quickly; we must ensure that our actions are also aligned with a deeper sense of purpose. In moments of uncertainty, it's easy to make decisions that feel immediate or convenient, but those decisions can often overlook their long-term impact.

---

[63] Bazerman, M. H., & Moore, D. A. (2013). *Judgment in managerial decision making* (8th ed.). Wiley.

This is where purposeful decision-making comes in. Purpose acts as our guiding star, helping us move beyond short-term fixes and directing our actions toward lasting, positive change. It's about making decisions that not only solve the problem in front of us but also consider the impact on the planet, the people around us, and future generations. When we make decisions grounded in purpose, even the smallest steps can ripple outward, creating long-term progress and positive outcomes.

We live in a world full of distractions: limited time, incomplete information, and competing priorities. We're constantly juggling deadlines, uncertainty, and external pressures. We don't always have the luxury of making perfect decisions. Herbert Simon's concept of "bounded rationality" helps us understand why. With the mental capacity, information, and time we have available, we rely on quick, practical decisions—what feels "good enough." [64] But here's the kicker: when we make decisions based only on what seems most efficient or immediate, we might miss opportunities to protect the planet and its people. We need to make quick decisions that solve the problem but also build a better world.

That's where purpose-driven leadership comes in. When you lead with a clear purpose, you have a compass to guide you. You can make quick decisions that prioritize the long-term impact on the Earth, people, and future generations. Purpose is a powerful motivator that drives you to make choices that align with your deeper values, even in the face of uncertainty. Leaders who are grounded in purpose make decisions that build a better world—not just for today, but for the future. And purpose-driven organizations, according to research,

---

[64] Simon, H. A. (1957). *Administrative behavior: A study of decision-making processes in administrative organizations* (2nd ed.). Free Press.

are better equipped to sustain long-term growth and create lasting impact.[65]

So, how can we make purposeful decisions when time is tight and information is scarce? First, we must accept that perfect decisions don't exist. The goal isn't flawless decision-making but purposeful action. Taking the best possible step with the information at hand and adjusting as we go.

Next, strengthen your decision-making process by gathering diverse perspectives. This helps you challenge assumptions and avoid falling into the trap of confirmation bias.[66] The more varied and reliable the sources of your information, the stronger and more sustainable your decisions will be.

The third step is to build habits that prioritize purpose over convenience. Instead of defaulting to what feels easiest or most familiar, we can create personal and organizational decision-making guidelines that align with our deeper values. For instance, companies committed to sustainability don't reflexively go with the cheapest suppliers; they build relationships with ethical partners who share their environmental and social impact goals. These habits ensure that even when we're making fast decisions, they're still anchored in what truly matters.

Finally, let's remember future generations in our decision-making process. Every choice we make, whether it's how we invest our resources, how we treat the environment, or how we design policies, has a ripple effect. Instead of focusing only on what's best for right now, we must also ask, "How will this decision affect those who come after us?" Research on intergenerational decision-making suggests that when people are reminded of their connection to future

---

[65] George, B., Sims, P., McLean, A. N., & Mayer, D. (2007). *Discovering your authentic leadership*. Harvard Business Review, 85(2), 129-138.

[66] Kahneman, D. (2011). *Thinking, fast and slow*. Farrar, Straus and Giroux.

generations, they make more ethical, sustainable choices. Integrating this mindset into your actions today will help build a better world for tomorrow.

## ART IS ACTION

It's easy to think that making a difference, especially for the planet, requires a background in fields like environmental science, sustainability, or policy. While these areas are crucial, they're not the only ones where change can happen. In fact, the arts play an essential role, too. Though they don't always get the same recognition as scientific discoveries or policy shifts, art influences culture, and culture shapes everything. How we see the world, how we treat each other, and how we care for our planet are all affected by what we create and share.

Think about it: most movements that brought about cultural change had art at its core. Stories, music, murals, poetry, all these contribute to how we assemble our histories, how we imagine what's possible, and how we connect with ideas that might otherwise feel too big or too overwhelming. The environmental movement itself was and is powered by art. Rachel Carson's *Silent Spring* was more than a book; it was a work of storytelling that made people feel the urgency of protecting nature. It was a call to arms. The haunting images of melting ice caps and deforested landscapes in photography exhibitions move people in ways data charts never could.

Activist art has this incredible way of making tough conversations impossible to ignore. Take Banksy, for example. Their street art isn't just about creating something cool to look at; it tackles big issues like climate change and corporate greed, sparking conversations that might have otherwise been avoided. Or think about Shepard Fairey's *We the People* series. It became a symbol of resistance and unity, especially during politically charged times. The series, with bold portraits of women, people of color, immigrants, and others, became a powerful reminder to stand up for social justice.

Then there's Agnes Denes, an artist who turns the land itself into her canvas. Her piece *Wheatfield: A Confrontation* transformed a garbage-strewn lot in Manhattan into a stunning field of wheat, sending a bold message about land use, sustainability, and what we really value as a society.

More recently, Maya Lin, the designer of the Vietnam Veterans Memorial, has turned her artistry toward the climate crisis with her *What is Missing?* project. This interactive piece highlights species extinction and habitat loss while encouraging people to share their own memories of the natural world, helping all of us connect to the Earth in a deeper way. And Andy Goldsworthy, who creates beautiful art with natural materials like stones, leaves, and ice, makes temporary pieces that remind us just how fragile and beautiful nature is.

These artists show us that art isn't just about looking at something pretty. It's about feeling something deep inside. Their work challenges us, gets us thinking, and, most importantly, it pushes us to act. Art can make big, abstract issues feel personal. When someone writes a song about a place they love, paints a picture of a better world, or makes a film about climate refugees, it doesn't just teach us. It makes us feel. And that feeling is what drives action.

Yes, we absolutely need scientists, policymakers, and conservationists. But we also need artists. People who share their stories, paint their visions, and create the emotional connections that inspire all of us to act. The best part? You don't need permission to make art. It doesn't have to be perfect. Just create. Art is action.

## HABITUAL ACTION

Taking action can be tough, especially when there's so much uncertainty and so many decisions to make. But here's the thing: the more we make action a habit, the easier it becomes. One way to do that is by setting decision-making rules that match our values. These guiding principles help us make decisions faster and with less stress.

Another key is to see risk not as something scary but as an opportunity to learn. Everyone makes mistakes. It's part of the journey. The real mistake is doing nothing at all. So, let's embrace that mindset of learning from setbacks and keep moving forward. If we're struggling to make decisions, one trick is to set time limits for ourselves. When we have too much time to think, we can get stuck in overthinking. But when we set deadlines, we tend to make quicker, often better decisions. Breaking big tasks into smaller, easier steps can also make things feel less overwhelming.

And, as we take action, we build momentum. Even small steps forward make a big difference, especially in a team. When leaders create a safe environment where people feel comfortable experimenting, the whole team becomes more action-oriented. People are much more likely to take the leap when they know they won't be punished for trying something new.

It's important to also consider the people in your circle. If you spend time with people who act, who try out ideas and push forward, you'll naturally pick up that habit. It's a bit like a snowball effect—creating momentum by just starting and staying accountable.

Instead of only measuring success by quick wins or reaching the finish line, it's important to celebrate progress. Small victories along the way can keep us motivated, even when we're working toward bigger goals.

The action we take today really does shape tomorrow. Whether it's in our personal lives, in business, or as leaders, every decision ripples forward. The future isn't built by waiting around—it's made by those who step forward and get to work.

Every day, I look at a quote from David Bowie hanging by my desk. It's my little reminder to stretch myself and take action: "If you feel safe in the area you're working in, you're not working in the right area. Always go a little further in the water than you feel you're capable of being in. Go a little bit out of your depth. And when you don't feel that your feet are quite touching the bottom, you're just about in the right place to do something exciting."

## TAKE THE LEAP

Waiting for the perfect moment? It's a myth. The leaders who make the biggest impact aren't the ones who have every single detail figured out ahead of time. They're the ones who take that first step anyway, even when they're unsure, and adjust as they go. When you're leading through fire and in complicated times, it's especially true.

The world is crying out for more of this kind of leadership. We need more people who will take action with purpose, create momentum even when things feel stuck, and choose courage over hesitation. Whether it's in business, activism, art, or community work, action is what moves ideas from being just possibilities into real, tangible outcomes. It's the spark that turns a dream into a movement, a solution into a revolution, and a quiet hope into something that can truly transform the world.

Action doesn't just happen by chance; it happens when it's intentional, when it's aligned with our deepest values, and when it takes into account the well-being of future generations. And that's when we leave the world better than we found it.

So here's your invitation: Take the leap. Step into the unknown. Move forward even when you feel like you're not sure where the ground is beneath you. Momentum isn't found in waiting. It's built when we take action. The future belongs to those who have the courage to take that big leap and start shaping it. As Joe Strummer once said, "The future is unwritten."

# KEY TAKEAWAYS

- **Action is the key to change.** Real progress comes when we move forward, even without a perfect plan. The leaders who make the biggest impact don't wait for the perfect moment. They take action, adapt as they go, and make things happen.

- **Dreams don't work unless you do.** It's easy to let dreams linger, waiting for the right time. But the truth is, they only come to life when we take that first step no matter how messy or imperfect it might be. Don't let fear or hesitation hold you back from turning your dreams into reality.

- **Overthinking holds us back.** We all get stuck in the trap of overthinking, weighing every decision until nothing gets done. The solution? Underthinking. Just take action, make the best decision you can, and adjust as you go.

- **Purpose guides us to better decisions.** In moments of uncertainty, decisions can be tough. But when we make them with purpose, we're more likely to make choices that are aligned with our values and the long-term impact we want to create.

- **The future is shaped by action today.** Every decision we make ripples out into the future. We need to take action with urgency and intention, always considering how our choices today will impact the world tomorrow.

# REFLECT ON ACTION

- What's a dream you've been putting off, and what's the first step you can take to bring it to life?

- How can you move past hesitation and take action, even when you don't have the whole plan figured out?

- Where in my life have you been overthinking a decision, and how can you make the next move without getting stuck in analysis?

- What values guide your decisions, and how can you make sure your actions are aligned with them?

- In what areas of your life can you embrace uncertainty and take action with purpose, even if the outcome is unknown?

- What's one small step you can take today to move toward the bigger goals you've set for myself or my community?

- How can you remind yourself that the choices you make today shape the world you want to see tomorrow?

# CHAPTER NINE

# THE JOY FACTOR: FINDING FULFILLMENT IN THE EVERYDAY

*I want to stand by the river in my finest dress. I want to sing, strong and hard, and stomp my feet with a hundred others so that the waters hum with our happiness. I want to dance for the renewal of the world.*

## — Robin Wall Kimmerer

There are times in life when joy comes easily: the laughter of a friend across the table, the first sip of coffee in the quiet morning, the way the sun stretches across the sky just before setting. And then there are times when joy feels like the most difficult thing to achieve, when the world appears to be unraveling, when exhaustion sets in, and when the weight of all that's broken feels too much.

But let's remember joy is not a reward we wait to deserve, nor is it a fragile thing that disappears when times are tough. It is a resource, a form of resilience, a candle we keep lit even when the wind howls.

Joy is an act of defiance in a world that often swoops in to try to steal it away. And in this chapter, we are going to talk about why joy matters. Why it is essential to our well-being, why it keeps us connected to our humanity, and why it's not just something we stumble upon but something we must actively create and protect.

## THE MOMENT I REALIZED I HAD STOPPED CELEBRATING

I wasn't always aware of the power of joy. For years, I moved fast. Too fast. My days blurred together in an endless rush of meetings, projects, deadlines. I would reach a milestone and immediately turn my attention to the next thing. A major achievement? No time to reflect. Just keep moving. Keep pushing. Keep proving.

Until one day, Char Sundust, my dear mentor and friend, asked a simple question that stopped me in my tracks:

*"When was the last time you celebrated a win?"* ☞

I opened my mouth to answer, but nothing came out. I honestly couldn't remember.

Nothing came to me. Not a single moment of gratitude, of acknowledgment for my achievements, of what I had overcome. I had been so focused on the future that I had forgotten to be in the present. And I knew right then that I had to change that.

Char reminded me that celebration isn't about self-indulgence. It's not about sitting back and saying, "Look at me, I did it." Celebration is a way to mark progress and remind yourself that even in a world full of challenges, you are still moving forward. It is a way to build momentum and keep yourself engaged in your work, in your relationships, and in your own life. Because if we don't take the time to acknowledge the good, we start to believe it doesn't exist.

## JOY BUILDS RESILIENCE

When I started making space for joy, even in the smallest ways, I noticed something profound: I was stronger for it. Not in the muscle-

and-grit sense but in the way that allowed me to better manage stress, setbacks, and uncertainty. I wasn't running on empty anymore. I had fuel.

Positive emotions play a huge role in building resilience. They give us the internal resources we need to adapt and recover, especially in difficult times. Barbara Fredrickson's broaden-and-build theory shows that positive emotions don't just lift our spirits; they expand our thinking, help us find creative solutions, and improve our decision-making.[67] Joy, in particular, makes us not just happier but more effective too. And when we're in the middle of a crisis, being effective is exactly what we need.

When we let ourselves experience joy, we give our nervous system a break. Our cortisol levels drop, reducing the wear and tear that chronic stress causes. Chronic stress is linked to increased inflammation, cardiovascular disease, and a weakened immune system. But here's the good news: positive emotions act as a buffer. [68] Engaging in joyful activities, whether through social connection, movement, music, or laughter, lowers inflammation and strengthens the immune response.[69] In other words, joy is protective.

Joy isn't just about feeling good in the moment; it's actually a powerful tool to help us bounce back. Studies show that when we regularly experience positive emotions, we're able to recover more quickly from stress and trauma. One study even found that people who nurture joy tend to regain their sense of purpose and agency faster, even after tough life events like job loss, grief, or global

---

[67] Fredrickson, B. L. (2001). The role of positive emotions in positive psychology: The broaden-and-build theory of positive emotions. *American Psychologist, 56*(3), 218–226.

[68] Cohen, S., Janicki-Deverts, D., & Miller, G. E. (2007). Psychological stress and disease. *JAMA*, 298(14), 1685–1687.

[69] Steptoe, A., & Wardle, J. (2011). Positive affect and health: A review of the psychological and biological mechanisms. *The Journal of Psychosomatic Research*, 71(6), 412–416.

crises.[70] Joy helps us build emotional strength, giving us the resilience we need to get through challenges and come out the other side stronger. It's like having an inner resource that fuels our ability to keep going when things get tough.

Wonder why when you're stressed, it's hard to be creative? When we're stuck in a state of stress, our thinking narrows. Our brains go into survival mode, search for threats, and focus only on what's immediately in front of us. But joy flips the switch. Experiencing positive emotions literally broadens our cognitive scope and helps us solve problems in more innovative ways—all without the stresses inherent to survival mode.[71] This is why some of our best ideas come when we're relaxed when we're laughing when we're not forcing an outcome but allowing ourselves to be present.

Think about that for a second.

We are often told to push through hard times. To grind. To hustle. To double down. But what if the answer wasn't more effort? What if it was more joy? What if celebrating, laughing, dancing were the things that made us stronger?

It's counterintuitive in a world that glorifies exhaustion. But joy is energy. Joy is resilience. And when the world feels overwhelming, joy is the very thing that helps us keep going.

## FINDING JOY IN SMALL MOMENTS

Once I understood this, I changed the way I moved through the world. I didn't overhaul my life overnight. I simply began noticing joy. The way the light hit my kitchen table in the morning, stretching

[70] Tugade, M., & Frederickson, B. (2004). *Resilient individuals use positive emotions to bounce back from negative emotional experiences. Journal of Personality and Social Psychology, 86(2),* 320-333.

[71] Isen, A. M. (1999). Positive affect. *Handbook of Cognition and Emotion,* 521-539.

long golden fingers across my coffee cup. The scent of fresh basil in the garden, bright and peppery, reminding me that some things will always grow back. That song that instantly transported me back to a happy time when the air was warm, the laughter easy, and the future felt wide open. These moments had always been there. I just hadn't been paying attention, so I started paying attention.

And then, I started creating joy.

I bought a ridiculous pair of glittery boots because they made me happy. Every time I wore them, I walked a little taller. I sent little texts to friends for no reason other than to make them smile, tiny messages in bottles tossed out into the world. I started walking outside more—not to get anywhere, not to achieve a step goal, just to be reminded of the way the world moves in seasons. The way the trees let go of their leaves without regret. The way the ocean keeps pulling in and out, steady and unconcerned. The way the birds always know when to return. It reminded me that change is natural, that we are not meant to hold on too tightly, and that life continues.

And I wasn't ignoring the hard stuff. I was still deeply engaged in my work, still pushing for progress, and still trying to solve big, complicated problems. But I realized something: shouldering the weight of the world wasn't beneficial or helpful. If I let the hard stuff consume everything, what was I fighting for? If I believed in a better future, shouldn't I be living as if that future was possible? I started to understand that joy wasn't a distraction. It was fuel and kept me going.

So, I let joy in even more, not as an escape but as a strategy. I danced in my kitchen, even on days when my heart felt heavy. I celebrated small wins, not because they were enough, but because they reminded me that progress is still possible. I let myself laugh, even in the midst of uncertainty, because joy isn't earned; it's freely given, and it's already in us despite the state of things around us.

# JOY AS AN ACT OF DEFIANCE

There is something radical about choosing joy in a world that often feels like it's falling apart.

I think about the people who have faced unimaginable hardships and still danced. The communities that have endured oppression still found ways to sing, paint, and gather in celebration. The activists, the caregivers, the people working at the frontlines of crisis who, even in the midst of exhaustion, still find moments to laugh. Or Oscar Wilde's humorous last words: "My wallpaper and I are fighting a duel to the death. One of us has to go."

Joy is not about ignoring pain. It is about refusing to let pain have the final say.

Viktor Frankl, a Holocaust survivor and the author of *Man's Search for Meaning* wrote about the power of finding meaning, even in the darkest places imaginable. He observed that in concentration camps, those who found a sense of purpose, a reason to live beyond the suffering, were more likely to survive. He famously wrote, "Everything can be taken from a man but one thing: the last of the human freedoms—to choose one's attitude in any given set of circumstances, to choose one's own way."

Frankl's insight is crucial: when we choose joy and create meaning, particularly in dire circumstances, we reclaim our freedom. This isn't denial, it's defiance. It says I *will not* let the darkness consume me. I *will not* let the fire destroy my spirit. I will dance, I will laugh, and I will love because that is how I stay human.

During the Civil Rights Movement, activists didn't just march and protest. They sang. They held onto their joy because they knew it was a source of strength. Indigenous cultures around the world have long understood that dance, music, and storytelling are not luxuries—they are survival tools and ways of keeping traditions alive.

Even in the environmental movement, joy plays a role. The poet and farmer Wendell Berry once wrote, "Be joyful though you have considered all the facts." Joy stokes the fight. It reminds us of what we are fighting for.

Berry reminds us that joy is not ignorance. It is not turning a blind eye to the injustices, the destruction, or the overwhelming weight of the world's problems. Instead, it is an insistence on living fully despite those realities. It is a call to hold both grief and gratitude in the same breath, to acknowledge what is broken while still reveling in what remains whole.

To be joyful, even after considering all the facts, is a radical act. You see the challenges, but you will not let it harden your heart. You see the challenges, but you will not let them steal your wonder at the beauty in the world.

## CULTIVATING JOY

Joy doesn't just happen. It's not something we stumble upon in rare, perfect moments. It's something we create, something we nurture, something we return to, especially when the world feels heavy. If we want joy in our lives, we must make space for it. We must be intentional about noticing it, inviting it in, and holding onto it, even when everything around us is telling us to focus on the struggle.

For a long time, I thought joy was something that came later. After the work was done and problems were solved. And after I had checked everything off my endless to-do list. But joy isn't a reward. It's a resource. And when I stopped waiting for it and started cultivating it in my daily life, I realized it made me stronger, more present, and ready to focus on the work that matters.

So how do we do that? How do we build joy into our lives, even when things feel hard?

We start by noticing. Joy is already around us—woven into the small, ordinary moments—but we have to train ourselves to see it. The way our scrappy rescue dog loses his mind with happiness every time we walk through the door. The rhythm of a song that makes us want to dance, even if just for a minute. These small invitations to joy are everywhere. We just have to slow down enough to catch them.

It turns out there's science behind this. Our brains are naturally wired to focus more on negative experiences. It is a survival mechanism that helped our ancestors stay alert to threats in the environment.[72] But the good news is that research also shows we're not stuck there. When we intentionally notice and savor joyful moments, we can actually begin to rewire our brains to look for the good.

How do we rewire it?

*We create joyful rituals.* Rituals help anchor us, so when we create rituals around joy, we make it a part of our daily rhythm. Maybe it's a morning tea that you drink slowly instead of rushing through. Maybe it's lighting a candle before bed, stretching in the afternoon, or keeping a journal. The ritual can be simple.

*We move our bodies in ways that feel good.* Movement and joy are deeply connected. When we move, we release endorphins, our body's natural mood boosters. But movement doesn't have to be about fitness goals or checklists. It can take the form of dancing in the kitchen, stretching, or taking a walk just to feel the air on your face. There are countless ways to move; the choice is yours. Studies show that even small amounts of movement improve mood and reduce stress.[73] The key is to find movement that brings you joy, not something that feels like another obligation.

---

[72] Baumeister, R. F., Bratslavsky, E., Finkenauer, C., & Vohs, K. D. (2001). Bad is stronger than good. *Review of General Psychology, 5*(4), 323-370.

[73] Ratey, J. J., & Hagerman, E. (2008). *Spark: The revolutionary new science of exercise and the brain.* Little, Brown.

*We make space for creativity.* Joy and creativity feed each other. You don't have to be an artist to create. Creativity can mean doodling in the margins of a notebook, painting a watercolor, writing a silly poem, or arranging your space in a way that makes you feel good. Engaging in creative activities increases positive emotions and reduces anxiety.[74] It doesn't have to be for anyone else. It doesn't have to be perfect. Just create something.

*We surround ourselves with people who lift us up.* Joy is contagious. The people we spend time with shape our emotional state. If we want more joy in our lives, we can make space for the people who bring it. Those who make us laugh, remind us of who we are, and celebrate our wins. Positive emotions spread through social networks.[75] So, if we want more joy, we need to seek out those who carry it.

*We make room for laughter.* Laughter is one of the simplest and most powerful ways to cultivate joy. It lowers stress hormones, boosts the immune system, and strengthens social bonds.[76] So, go ahead, watch a comedy, read a funny book, and tell those ridiculous stories from your life. Laugh even when things feel hard—especially when things feel hard.

*We practice gratitude.* Practicing gratitude ensures we also recognize what's good in our lives—and in the lives of others. Writing down a few things you're thankful for each day has incredible benefits, like

---

[74] Conner, T. S., DeYoung, C. G., & Silvia, P. J. (2018). Everyday creative activity as a path to flourishing. *The Journal of* Fowler, J. H., & Christakis, N. A. (2008).

[75] Fowler, J. H., & Christakis, N. A. (2008). Dynamic spread of happiness in a large social network: Longitudinal analysis over 20 years in the Framingham Heart Study. *BMJ, 337*, a2338.

[76] Bennett, M. P., & Lengacher, C. (2009). Humor and laughter may influence health: III. Laughter and health outcomes. *Evidence-Based Complementary and Alternative Medicine, 6*(2), 159-164.

increasing happiness levels and reducing depressive symptoms.[77] The trick is to be specific. Instead of writing, "I'm grateful for my friends," try, "I'm grateful for the way my best friend sent me that ridiculous meme today when she knew I needed a laugh." Small details make gratitude feel real.

*We let go of guilt around joy.* So many of us feel like we have to earn joy. That we have to finish all our work, solve all the world's problems, and fix everything before we're allowed to be happy. But joy is not a betrayal of struggle. It is what allows us to keep going. As Audre Lorde wrote, "Caring for myself is not self-indulgence. It is self-preservation, and that is an act of political warfare." Choosing joy is not selfish. It is necessary.

Joy doesn't just happen. We build it. We cultivate it. We choose it again and again. Start small but start today. And remember: Joy is your birthright. It is always there, waiting for you to claim it.

## KEY TAKEAWAYS

- **Joy is not a luxury; it's a survival skill.** In hard times, joy isn't a reward we earn. It's a resource we can draw from to build resilience, hope, and strength.

- **Celebration keeps us moving forward.** Marking progress, no matter how small helps remind us that we are growing, changing, and still moving toward something better.

- **Joy makes us stronger, not weaker.** Positive emotions like joy lower our stress, fuel creativity, boost our immune system, and help us bounce back faster from life's challenges.

---

[77] Emmons, R. A., & McCullough, M. E. (2003). Counting blessings versus burdens: An experimental investigation of gratitude and subjective well-being in daily life. *Journal of Personality and Social Psychology, 84*(2), 377-389.

- **Joy is a practice, not an accident.** It's something we cultivate intentionally by noticing small moments, creating rituals, laughing often, and surrounding ourselves with what lifts us up.

- **Choosing joy is an act of courage.** In a world full of heartbreak and uncertainty, making room for joy isn't denial. It's a radical, life-affirming choice to stay human, hopeful, and engaged.

# REFLECT ON JOY

- When was the last time you truly celebrated a win—big or small—and how did it feel to pause and recognize it?

- In your daily life, where are you rushing past small moments of joy without noticing? How can you slow down and catch more of them?

- How do you tend to view joy—do you see it as a bonus or as something essential to your well-being?

- What small, joyful rituals could you build into your days to anchor yourself, even during stressful times?

- Who in your life lifts your spirit just by being themselves? How can you make more intentional space for those relationships?

- When was a time that joy gave you the strength to keep going through something hard? What can that memory teach you now?

- How can you use joy as a fuel for the work, love, and change you want to create in the world?

# CLOSING THOUGHTS

# THE JOURNEY CONTINUES: A BLUEPRINT FOR RESILIENT LEADERSHIP

Leadership today requires us to think beyond the status quo. It means navigating the fast, messy, sometimes beautiful changes happening all around us. It means finding the steady ground within ourselves while the world reshapes itself at record speed.

If you've made it this far in the book, I want to pause and acknowledge you. You're not here by accident. You're someone who cares deeply about the future and is willing to do the hard work to help build it. That matters more than you know.

Throughout these chapters, we've explored what it means to lead through fire. We talked about staying rooted in purpose, leading with compassion, striving for excellence (not perfection), building bridges, making wise decisions in a noisy world, speaking with courage, acting boldly even when the path is unclear, seeking win-win solutions, and nurturing resilience and joy along the way.

Leadership now can feel difficult. If you're having challenges, you are not alone. The world is facing real challenges—climate change, technological disruption, and deep social shifts. Inside every challenge, there's a chance to lead differently. To lead better. To shape something new.

Leadership in this moment demands something deeper. It calls for resilience that's rooted and flexible. It asks us to stay grounded even as we adapt. It reminds us to stay hopeful, even when the road ahead looks uncertain.

## YOUR BLUEPRINT FOR RESILIENT LEADERSHIP

So, where do you go from here? How do you keep leading through fire when the winds pick up again?

Here's a blueprint—a set of guideposts you can come back to any time you need to find your footing:

- **Stay rooted in your purpose.** Purpose is your compass. It's what keeps you steady when the waves crash around you. Keep it close. Let it guide your decisions, especially when things feel uncertain.

- **Lead with compassion—for yourself and others.** Strong leadership isn't about powering through, no matter the cost. It's about knowing when to listen, when to rest, and when to extend grace. Compassion fuels resilience.

- **Embrace imperfection, strive for excellence.** Forget perfection. It's a mirage. Excellence is a practice. Keep learning, keep growing, and trust that progress matters more than getting everything exactly right.

- **Practice discernment with courage and clarity.** Not every voice deserves equal weight. Slow down. Weigh what is true. Lead thoughtfully, not reactively.

- **Speak with courage and honesty.** Real leadership creates spaces where truth can rise, hard conversations can happen, and trust can deepen.

- **Build bridges.** True change doesn't happen in isolation. It happens in the community. Surround yourself with people who challenge and inspire you. Invest in cooperation over competition.

- **Seek win-win solutions.** The best leadership lifts everyone. Seek paths where collective good outweighs short-term wins.

- **Take bold, imperfect action.** Waiting for the perfect plan is another way fear tries to keep us small. Step forward anyway. Start before you're ready. The path reveals itself as you move.

- **Choose joy, even on a bad day.** Joy isn't a distraction—it's survival fuel. Celebrate small wins. Laugh often. Hold onto the beauty that reminds you why the fight for a better future is worth it.

# THE FUTURE IS YOURS TO SHAPE

We are living through a defining moment. The old ways of doing things are no longer enough. That doesn't have to be a reason to despair. It can be an invitation—to imagine something better. To lead in ways that are more courageous, more compassionate, and more sustainable. To build a future that reflects the values we know are possible: dignity, justice, creativity, and love.

You don't need to be perfect. You don't need to have all the answers. You simply need to stay rooted, stay open, and keep stepping forward.

The world needs leaders who are willing to move through uncertainty with hope. Leaders who don't run from the fire—but who walk through it, carrying something better on the other side. You are one of those leaders. And you are exactly where you're meant to be. Let's build a better world together. Let's lead through fire—and into the future—with courage, resilience, and joy.

Joe Strummer said that "the future is unwritten." Let's write a better future together.

With deep gratitude and unwavering hope,

— *Brenna*

# A GIFT FOR YOU

I'm so grateful you spent time with this book.

As a thank you, I'd love to offer you a little something to keep the momentum going.

You can download the *Purpose Power Worksheet* — a set of thoughtful prompts and ideas to help you discover, deepen, or redefine your purpose — whenever you're ready. Just head to the link below.

I hope it supports you as you continue to walk your path.

www.brennadavis.com

# ACKNOWLEDGMENTS

To my husband: Your love, steady encouragement, and unwavering support have been my anchor. I am forever grateful.

To every one of my grandmothers: Courageous, brave, sassy, and as loving as they come. Your strength and love live on in me.

To my mother, Jude: You showed me how to move through the world without getting trapped in its rigid lines.

To my father, JohnCarl: Thank you for the gift of the power of words that can shape a better world.

To Sun Bear: Thank you for giving me my first ecology lesson and for opening my eyes to the deep, beautiful interconnection of life.

To Char Sundust: Thank you for helping me hear my own heart more clearly and walk my path with courage and grace.

To David Bowie: Thank you for showing me that real magic happens when you go a little deeper into the water than you think you're capable of.

To Izdihar Jamil, PHD: Thank you for teaching me how to break through, and for helping me believe that this book could live in the world.

To all my mentors, my friends, and everyone I've had the privilege to learn from: This book is as much yours as it is mine.

# ABOUT THE AUTHOR

Brenna Davis is an environmental scientist, regenerative business leader, and CEO of the nation's leading Perpetual Purpose Trust-owned company. She brings more than two decades of experience advancing sustainability, inclusive leadership, and alternative ownership models across seven industries. Brenna has advised national policy, appeared on every major news network, and contributed to climate policy work at the highest levels. She has a B.S. in Environmental Science from Western Washington University and an M.S. in Business Management from Antioch University, as well as graduate certificates in Systems Thinking and Theory, Creative Change, and Leadership. She is a lifelong student of cross-cultural shamanism. She has contributed to a number of best-selling leadership anthologies and is the author of *Leading Through Fire: Resilient Leadership for People, Planet, and the Future*, a field guide for conscious leadership in times of disruption. Find out more at brennadavis.com.

www.brennadavis.com

www.ingramcontent.com/pod-product-compliance
Lightning Source LLC
Chambersburg PA
CBHW032048090426
42744CB00004B/119